Mountain Biking
Portland

SCOTT RAPP

FALCON® Guilford, Connecticut
An imprint of The Globe Pequot Press

Copyright © 2001 by The Globe Pequot Press

Cover photo by Karl Weatherly/Index Stock.

Library of Congress Cataloging-in-Publication Data
Rapp, Scott, 1969-
    Mountain biking Portland/Scott Rapp.
       p. cm.
    ISBN 1-56044-916-0
       1. All terrain cycling—Oregon—Portland Region—Guidebooks. 2. Portland Region (Or.)—Guidebooks. I. Title.
    GV1045.5.O72 P677 2001
    917.95´490444—dc21

                                                                    00-050320

 Text pages printed on recycled paper.

Manufactured in the United States of America
First Edition/First Printing

Contents

Get Ready to Crank!

West of Portland

In Portland

Molalla River Corridor

Mount Hood Area

Vancouver Area

Mount St. Helens

Acknowledgments

Thanks to Amy and Henry for joining me during most of the research for this book.

Overview Map

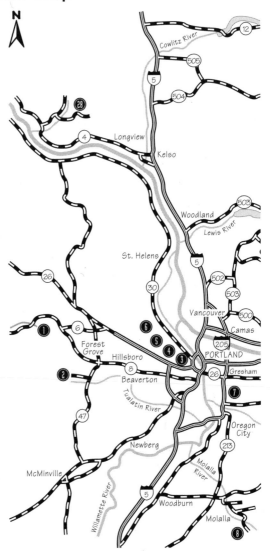

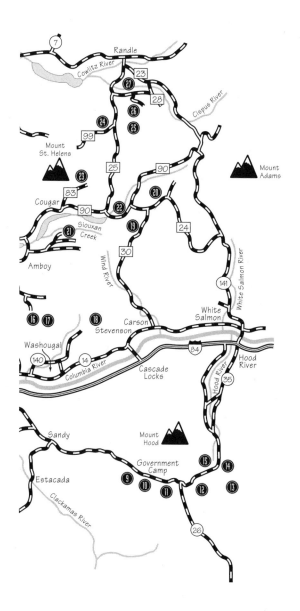

Legend

Interstate		Campground	
U.S. Highway		Picnic Area	
State or Other Principal Road		Buildings	
Forest Service Road		Peak/Elevation	4,507 ft.
Interstate Highway		Elevation	x 4,507 ft.
Paved Road		Gate	
Gravel Road		Parking Area	
Unimproved Road		Overlook/Viewpoint	
Trail (singletrack)		Mine	
Trailhead		Cliffs/Bluff	
Trail Marker		Ski Lift	
Waterway		Forest Boundary	
Intermittent Waterway		Map Orientation	N
Lake/Reservoir		Scale	0 0.5 1 MILES
Meadow/Swamp			

Get Ready to Crank!

Where to ride? It's a quandary that faces every mountain biker, beginner or expert, local or expatriate.

If you're new to the area, where do you start? If you're a longtime local, how do you avoid the rut of riding the same old trails week after week? And how do you find new terrain that's challenging but not overwhelming? Or an easier ride for when your not-so-serious buddies want to come along?

Welcome to *Mountain Biking Portland*. Here are twenty-eight rides ranging from easy road routes to smooth single-track to bravado-busting boulder fields. The rides are described in plain language, with accurate distances and ratings for physical and technical difficulty. Each entry offers a wealth of detailed information that's easy to read and use, from an armchair or on the trail.

Our aim here is three-fold: to help you choose a ride that's appropriate for your fitness and skill level; to make it easy to find the trailhead; and to help you complete the ride safely, without getting lost. Take care of these basics and fun is bound to break loose.

Portland's Geography:
What to Expect

The rides in this book cover a wide variety of terrain. But most of the rides are mountainous, exposed, or both, and that means two things: They can be steep and rough, and inclement weather is always a threat.

Mountain terrain requires preparedness. Get in good shape before you attempt any of these rides, and know your limits. Keep your bike running smoothly with frequent cleaning and maintenance. Do a quick check before each ride to ensure that tires, rims, brakes, handlebars, seat, shifters, derailleurs, and chain all survived the last ride intact and are functioning properly.

Always carry at least one water bottle, though two are recommended (and don't forget to fill them). A snack, such as fruit or sports energy bars, will help keep those mighty thighs cranking for many hours. Dress for the weather and pack a wind- and waterproof jacket whenever there's any doubt. Don't forget sunglasses, sunscreen, lip balm, and insect repellent, as needed.

I tend to go light on tools, with a pump, spare tube, a small multitool, and some duct tape. This extra pound of gear could make the difference between arriving home a few minutes late and spending the night out on the trail. Some folks aren't comfortable unless they take 20 pounds of tools; you can usually hear them jangling up the trail, but they rarely get stranded by mechanical problems.

This book is designed to be easily carried along in a jersey pocket or bike bag, and the maps and ride descriptions will help anyone unfamiliar with the trails. For more detailed maps check out *Mountain Biking Greater Portland* or *Mountain Biking Southwest Washington* from Fat Tire

Publications, which provide topographical maps to accompany descriptions of each ride.

Cycling gloves are another essential piece of safety equipment—saving hands from cuts and bruises from falls and encroaching branches and rocks. They also improve your grip and comfort on the handlebars. Finally, always wear a helmet; it can save your life.

Portland's weather spans the gamut of North American extremes, particularly in the surrounding mountains. Snow can fall any day of the year, but summer highs may top 100 degrees F. In general, higher elevations are cooler (by as much as 10 degrees for every 1,000 feet gained) and windier. If you are driving to a trailhead, play it safe and take a variety of clothes in the car to match the weather you may encounter. Summer and early fall are typically dry, with late fall, winter, and spring being much wetter and cooler. This is a general rule, so be sure to check weather forecasts before heading out.

Many of Portland's rides are open year-round. While people are skiing on Mount Hood 60 miles away, bikers are playing in the mud on one of many lowland trails near town.

The soil near Portland and on the west slope of the Cascade Mountains has a high clay content that usually turns muddy in late October and doesn't really dry out until June. This being said, a lot of rides are open year-round, but you should expect to get muddy and budget extra time for cleaning your bike after the ride. Stay off singletrack trails when they are wet and muddy; riding trails in these conditions hastens erosion and leaves deep ruts.

The yearly number of rainy or snowy days tends to increase the closer you go to the Cascade Range. While rain may be falling in Portland, the Pioneer Bridle Trail could be under 8 feet of snow. It's best to check with land managers on the condition of trails before heading out for a ride.

Rules of the Trail

If every mountain biker always yielded the right-of-way, stayed on the trail, avoided wet or muddy trails, never cut switchbacks, never skidded, always rode in control, showed respect for other trail users, and carried out every last scrap of what was carried in (candy wrappers and bike-part debris included)—in short, *did the right thing*—we wouldn't need a list of rules governing our behavior.

Fact is, most mountain bikers are conscientious and *are* trying to do the right thing. Most of us own that integrity. (No one becomes good at something as demanding and painful as grunting up sheer mountainsides by cheating.)

Most of us don't need rules.

But we do need knowledge. What exactly is the right thing to do?

Here are some guidelines—I like to think of them as reminders—reprinted by permission from the International Mountain Bicycling Association (IMBA). The basic theme is to reduce or eliminate any damage to the land and water, the plant and wildlife inhabitants, and other backcountry visitors and trail users. Ride with respect.

IMBA Rules of the Trail

Thousands of miles of dirt trails have been closed to mountain bicyclists, including some in central Oregon. The irresponsible riding habits of a few riders have been a factor.

Do your part to maintain trail access by observing the following rules of the trail, formulated by IMBA, whose mission is to promote environmentally sound and socially responsible mountain biking.

1. Ride on open trails only. Respect trail and road closures (ask if not sure), avoid possible trespass on private land, obtain permits and authorization as may be required. Federal and state wilderness areas are closed to cycling, so the way you ride will influence trail management decisions and policies.

2. Leave no trace. Be sensitive to the dirt beneath you. Even on open (legal) trails, you should not ride under conditions where you will leave evidence of your passing, such as on certain soils after a rain. Recognize different types of soil and trail construction; practice low-impact cycling. This also means staying on existing trails and not creating any new ones. Be sure to pack out at least as much as you pack in.

3. Control your bicycle! Inattention for even a second can cause problems. Obey all bicycle speed regulations and recommendations.

4. Always yield trail. Make known your approach well in advance. A friendly greeting (or bell) is considerate and works well; don't startle others. Show your respect when passing by slowing to a walking pace or even stopping. Anticipate other trail users around corners or in blind spots.

5. Never spook animals. All animals are startled by an unannounced approach, a sudden movement, or a loud noise. This can be dangerous for you, others, and the animals. Give animals extra room and time to adjust to you. When passing horses use special care and follow directions from the horseback riders (ask if uncertain). Running cattle and disturbing wildlife is a serious offense. Leave gates as you found them, or as marked.

6. Plan ahead. Know your equipment, your ability, and the area in which you are riding—and prepare accordingly. Be self-sufficient at all times, keep your equipment in good repair, and carry necessary supplies for changes in weather or other conditions. A well-executed trip is a satisfaction to you and not a burden or offense to others. Always wear a helmet.

Keep trails open by setting a good example of environmentally sound and socially responsible off-road cycling.

How to Use This Guide

Mountain Biking Portland describes twenty-eight mountain bike rides in their entirety. Many of the featured rides are loops, beginning and ending at the same point but coming and going on different trails. Loops are by far the most popular type of ride, and Portlanders are fortunate to have so many near town.

Be forewarned, however: the difficulty of a loop ride may change dramatically depending on which direction you ride around the loop. If you are unfamiliar with the rides in this book, try them first as described here. The directions follow the path of least resistance (which does not necessarily mean "easy"). After you've been over the terrain, you can determine whether a given loop would be fun—or even feasible—in the reverse direction.

Portions of some rides follow gravel and even paved roads, and a handful of rides never wander off road. Purists may wince at road rides in a book about mountain biking, but these are special rides. They offer a chance to enjoy mountain scenery and fresh air while covering easier, non-technical terrain for people new to the sport. They can also be used by hard-core riders on "active rest" days or when higher elevation trails are closed by mud or snow.

Each ride description in this book follows the same format:

Number and name of the ride: Rides are cross referenced by number throughout this book. In many cases, parts of rides or entire routes can be linked to other rides for longer trips or variations on a standard route. These opportunities are noted, followed by "see Ride(s)."

For the names of rides I relied on official names of trails, roads, and natural features as shown on national forest and U.S. Geological Survey maps, though several trails in this guide are new and do not appear on these maps.

Location: The general whereabouts of the ride; distance and direction from Portland or, in some cases, Vancouver.

Distance: The length of the ride in miles, given as a loop, one way, or round trip.

Time: An estimate of how long it takes to complete the ride. *The time listed is the actual riding time and does not include rest stops.* Strong, skilled riders may be able to do a given ride in less than the estimated time, whereas other riders may take considerably longer. Also bear in mind that severe weather, changes in trail conditions, or mechanical problems may prolong a ride.

Tread: The type of road or trail: paved road, gravel road, dirt road or jeep track, doubletrack, ATV-width singletrack, and singletrack.

Aerobic level: The level of physical effort required to complete the ride: easy, moderate, or strenuous. See the explanation of the rating systems on page 10.

Technical difficulty: The level of bike handling skills needed to complete the ride upright and in one piece. Technical difficulty is rated on a scale from 1 to 5, with 1 being the easiest (see the explanation of the rating systems on page 12).

Hazards: A list of dangers that may be encountered on a ride, including traffic, weather, trail obstacles and conditions, risky stream crossings, difficult route-finding, and other perils. Remember: Conditions may change at any time. Be alert for storms, new fences, downfall, missing trail signs, and mechanical failure. Fatigue, heat, cold, and/or dehydration may impair judgment. Always wear a helmet and other safety equipment. Ride in control at all times.

Highlights: Special features or qualities that make a ride worth doing (as if we needed an excuse!): scenery, fun singletrack, access to other routes, chances to see wildlife, the list goes on.

Land status: A list of managing agencies or landowners. Always leave gates as you found them and respect the land, regardless of who owns it.

Maps: A list of available maps.

Access: How to find the trailhead or the start of the ride. Several rides can be pedaled right from town; for others it's best to drive to the trailhead.

The ride: A mile-by-mile list of key points—landmarks, notable climbs and descents, obstacles, hazards, major turns and junctions—along the ride. All distances were measured to the tenth of a mile with a cyclo-computer (a bike-mounted odometer). Terrain, riding technique, and even tire pressure can affect odometer readings, so treat all mileages as estimates.

One last reminder—the real world is changing all the time. The information presented here is as accurate and up-to-date as possible, but there are no guarantees out in the mountains. You alone are responsible for your safety and for the choices you make on the trail.

If you do find an error or omission in this book, or a new and noteworthy change in the field, I'd like to hear from you. Please write to Scott Rapp, c/o The Globe Pequot Press, P.O. Box 480, Guilford, CT 06437.

Rating the Rides—One Person's Pain Is Another's Pleasure

One of the first lessons learned by most mountain bikers is to not trust their friends' accounts of how easy or difficult a given ride may be.

"Where ya wanna' ride today?"

"Let's do 'the Wall' dudes—it's gnarly in the middle, but even my grandma could fly up that last hill, and the view is way cool."

If you don't read between the lines, only painful experience will tell you that granny won the pro-elite class in last weekend's hillclimb race and "the view" is over the handlebars from the lip of a 1,000-foot drop on that fun little gnarly stretch.

So how do you know what you're getting into, before it's too late?

Don't always listen to your friends.

But do read this book. Mountain Biking guides from Falcon rate each ride for two types of difficulty: the *physical effort* required to pedal the distance, and the level of *bike-handling skills* needed to stay upright and make it home in one piece. We call these aerobic level and technical difficulty.

The following sections explain what the various ratings mean in plain, specific language. An elevation profile accompanies each ride description to help you determine how easy or hard the ride is. Be sure to weigh other factors such as elevation above sea level, total trip distance, weather and wind, and current trail conditions.

Aerobic Level Ratings

Bicycling is often touted as a relaxing, low-impact, relatively easy way to burn excess calories and maintain a healthy heart and lungs. Mountain biking, however, tends to pack a little more work (and excitement) into the routine.

Fat tires and soft or rough trails increase the rolling resistance, so it takes more effort to push those wheels around. And unpaved or off-road hills tend to be steeper than grades measured and tarred by the highway department. When we use the word *steep*, we mean a sweat-inducing, oxygen-sucking, lactose-building climb. If it's followed by an exclamation point—steep (!)—expect some honest pain on the way up (and maybe for days afterward).

So expect to breathe hard and sweat some, probably a lot. Pedaling around town is a good start, but it won't fully prepare you for the workout offered by most of these rides. If you're unsure of your level of fitness, see a doctor for a physical exam before tackling any of the rides in this book. And if you're riding to get back in shape or just for the fun of it, take it easy. Walk or rest if need be. Start with short rides and add on miles gradually.

Here's how we rate the exertion level for terrain covered in this book:

Easy: Flat or gently rolling terrain. No steeps or prolonged climbs.

Moderate: Some hills. Climbs may be short and fairly steep or long and gradual.

Strenuous: Frequent or prolonged climbs steep enough to require riding in the lowest gear; requires a high level of aerobic fitness, power, and endurance (typically acquired through many hours of riding and proper training). Less fit riders may need to walk.

Many rides are mostly easy and moderate but may have short strenuous sections. Other rides are mostly strenuous and should be attempted only after a complete medical checkup and implant of a second heart, preferably a big one. Also be aware that flailing through a highly technical section can be exhausting even on the flats. Good riding skills and a relaxed stance on the bike save energy.

Finally, any ride can be strenuous if you ride it hard and fast. Conversely, the pain of a lung-burning climb grows easier to tolerate as your fitness level improves. Learn to pace yourself and remember to schedule easy rides and rest days into your calendar.

Technical Difficulty Ratings

While you're pushing up that steep, strenuous slope, wondering how much farther you can go before your lungs prolapse and billow out of your mouth like an air bag in a desperate gasp for oxygen, remember that the dry heaves aren't the only hurdle on the way to the top of the mountain.

There's that tree across the trail, or the sideslope full of ball-bearing–sized pebbles, or the place where the trail disappears except for faint bits of rubber clinging to the smooth, sheer wall of lava straight ahead.

Mountain bikes will roll over or through an amazing array of life's little challenges, but sometimes we, as riders, have to help. Or at least close our eyes and hang on. As a last resort, some riders get off their bikes and walk—get this—before they flip over the handlebars. These folks have no sense of adventure. The rest of us hop onto our bikes with only the dimmest inkling of what lies ahead. And later we brag about the ride to hell (leaving out the part about carrying our bikes half the distance because hell has some highly technical terrain).

No more. The technical difficulty ratings in this book help take the worst surprises out of backcountry rides. In the privacy of your own home you can make an honest appraisal of your bike-handling skills and then find rides in these pages that are within your ability.

We rate technical difficulty on a scale from 1 to 5, from easiest to most difficult and have tried to make the ratings as objective as possible by considering the type of obstacles and their frequency of occurrence. The same standards were applied consistently through all the rides.

We've also added plus (+) and minus (-) symbols to cover gray areas between given levels of difficulty: a 4+ obstacle is harder than a 4, but easier than a -5. A stretch of trail rated as 5+ would be unrideable by all but the most skilled (or luckiest) riders.

Here are the 5 levels defined:

Level 1: Smooth tread; road or doubletrack; no obstacles, ruts, or steeps. Requires basic bike riding skills.

Level 2: Mostly smooth tread; wide, well-groomed singletrack or road/doubletrack with minor ruts or loose gravel or sand.

Level 3: Irregular tread with some rough sections; single or doubletrack with obvious route choices; some steep sections; occasional obstacles may include small rocks, roots, water bars, ruts, loose gravel or sand, and sharp turns or broad, open switchbacks.

Level 4: Rough tread with few smooth places; singletrack or rough doubletrack with limited route choices; steep sections, some with obstacles; obstacles are numerous and varied, including rocks, roots, branches, ruts, sidehills, narrow tread, loose gravel or sand, and switchbacks.

Level 5: Continuously broken, rocky, root-infested, or trenched tread; singletrack or extremely rough doubletrack with few route choices; frequent, sudden, and severe changes in gradient; some slopes so steep that wheels lift off ground; obstacles are nearly continuous and may include boulders, logs, water, large holes, deep ruts, ledges, piles of loose gravel, steep sidehills, encroaching trees, and tight switchbacks.

Most of the rides cover varied terrain, with an ever-changing degree of technical difficulty. Some trails run smooth with only occasional obstacles, and other trails are seemingly all obstacle. The path of least resistance, or line, is where you find it. In general, most obstacles are more challenging if you encounter them while climbing than while descending. On the other hand, in heavy surf (e.g., boulder fields, tangles of downfall, cliffs), fear plays a larger role when facing downhill.

Realize, too, that different riders have different strengths and weaknesses. Some folks can scramble over logs and boulders without a grunt, but they crash head over heels on every switchback turn. Some fly off the steepest drops and others freeze. Some riders climb like the wind and others just blow, and walk.

The key to overcoming "technical difficulties" is practice: Keep trying. Follow a rider who makes it look easy, and don't hesitate to ask for constructive criticism. Try shifting your weight (good riders move a lot, front to back, side to side, and up and down) and experimenting with balance and momentum. Find a smooth patch of lawn and practice riding as slowly as possible, even balancing at a standstill in a "track stand" (described in the Glossary). This will give you more confidence—and more time to recover or bail out—the next time the trail rears up and bites.

Historic Hiking Trail

Location: 37 miles west of Portland.

Distance: 8-mile loop.

Time: 1.5 to 3 hours.

Tread: 7.3 miles singletrack; 0.7 mile doubletrack.

Season: Summer and fall.

Aerobic level: Moderate to strenuous; short, steep climbs.

Technical difficulty: 4; tight corners, steep descents, and slick roots.

Hazards: This is a highly technical trail with several short, steep climbs and root-covered descents. Fording Devil's Fork Creek in the spring or after a period of prolonged rain can be dangerous and is always cold. Be aware that this area is popular with motorized users.

Highlights: Great singletrack, University Falls, and lush forest.

Land status: Tillamook State Forest.

Maps: *Mountain Biking Greater Portland*—Fat Tire Publications; USGS Roaring Creek, Timber .

•Historic Hiking Trail

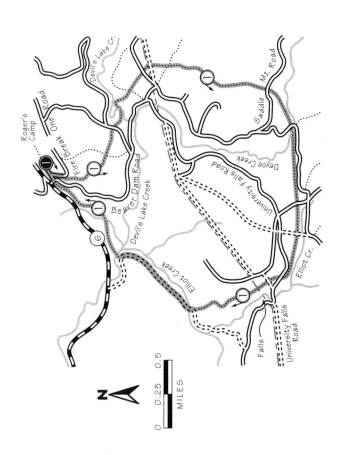

Access: From Portland take U.S. Highway 26 west for 20 miles to Oregon Highway 6. Go west on OR 6 for 17 miles to the summit and the access road to Roger's Camp on the left.

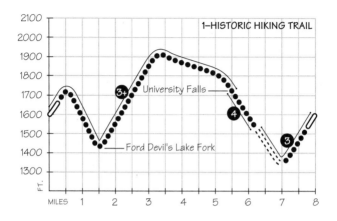

The Ride

0.0 From the parking area at Roger's Camp head uphill on the gravel Fire Break One Road. Find the Historic Hiking Trail beginning on the right, and take it as it climbs steeply.

0.2 Cross an ATV trail.

0.4 Trail forks; stay left.

0.55 Junction with an ATV trail; stay left.

0.6 Cross a gravel road.

1.0 The trail crosses another gravel road and begins a steep descent to Devil's Lake Creek.

1.2 Ford Devil's Lake Creek (use caution and prepare to get wet and cold up to at least your knees), and begin climbing steeply out of this small canyon.

1.5 Cross ATV trail.

1.9 Cross gravel road.

2.0 Trail crosses a doubletrack road that runs under some power lines.

2.2 Cross ATV trail.

2.5 Cross ATV trail.

3.3 Trail joins a gravel road to the right and then begins again on the left.

3.7 Cross gravel road.

3.8 Cross creek.

4.3 Cross gravel road.

4.6 Cross ATV trail.

5.1 Cross gravel road.

5.2 Cross ATV trail and begin descending steeply to University Falls.

5.4 Trail junction to University Falls. Follow the trail on the left to the University Falls viewpoint. As you continue, the trail will begin to descend steeply in places with many loose roots and rocks.

6.2 Bridge over Elliot Creek; junction with wide ATV trail (this bridge can be extremely slick when wet).

6.9 Cross a bridge and turn right onto a smaller ATV trail, which traverses a small meadow and then begins climbing steeply.

7.6 Reach a large gravel yard, circumvent the yard, and take the gravel road, which goes uphill to Roger's Camp.

8.0 End at Roger's Camp.

Henry Hagg Lake Trail

Location: 28 miles west of Portland.

Distance: 14.5-mile loop.

Time: 1.5 to 3.5 hours.

Tread: 12.4 miles singletrack; 2.1 miles pavement.

Season: Summer and fall.

Aerobic level: Moderate; short, steep climbs.

Technical difficulty: 3; tight corners and a few roots.

Hazards: Avoid riding this trail when the ground is wet; the wooden bridges become very slick. This is a popular hiking trail, so watch for traffic on the road portions of the loop. Expect to pay an entrance fee.

Highlights: Fun trail, deep forest, and views of the lake.

Land status: Washington County Parks.

Maps: *Mountain Biking Greater Portland*—Fat Tire Publications; USGS Gales Creek, Gaston.

Access: From Portland drive 22 miles west on Oregon Highway 8 to Forest Grove, then head 4 miles south on OR 47 to Scoggins Valley Road on the right. Follow this for 2 miles to the park entrance. Go left on West Shore Drive across the dam 0.7 mile to a large parking area on the right.

•Henry Hagg Lake Trail

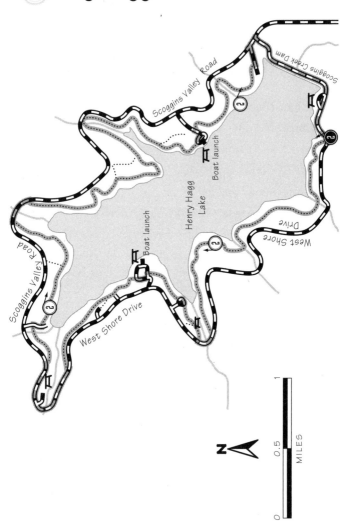

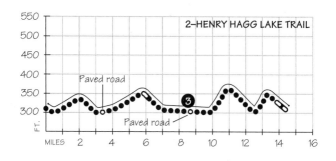

The Ride

0.0 Begin by riding clockwise on West Shore Drive.

0.2 Find trail on right, marked by a red steel post. Begin a fun roller-coaster section of singletrack.

1.2 Trail junction; go left, then right.

1.4 Trail enters a field then climbs gently.

1.7 Back into the woods.

2.2 Cross a small bridge, then begin climbing steeply to a sharp left at the top.

2.6 Enter another grassy field.

2.8 Reenter the forest.

3.4 Intersect a paved road (West Shore Drive); go right over a bridge.

3.5 Trail begins again on the right (marked by red post).

3.6 Continue straight at trail intersection.

3.65 Trail junction; stay right.

3.8 Trail becomes paved through picnic area.

3.9 Trail turns to dirt again (marked by red post).

4.2 Enter boat ramp/picnic area and ride across the parking area to the far side.

4.4 Trail begins again on far side of parking area (marked by red post).

4.9 Jog left then right at intersections (uphill goes back to the road).

5.1 Trail junction, go right, downhill.

5.5 Trail touches road.

5.7 Join West Shore Drive; go right.

6.0 Scoggins Creek Picnic Area on right, continue along the road.

6.3 Trail begins again on the right (marked by red post).

6.7 After crossing a short bridge, veer right.

6.8 Junction with gravel road, go right on the gravel road for a very short distance to the trail, which begins again on the left.

7.5 Trail junction at bench; stay right.

8.3 Trail junctions with Scoggins Valley Road; go right.

8.5 Trail begins again on the right (marked by a red post).

9.0 Stay right at a trail junction.

9.4 Stay right at a trail junction.

9.7 Continue straight at a trail junction.

9.8 Stay right at a trail junction.

10.1 Continue straight at a trail junction.

11.0 Trail touches road.

11.8 Continue straight (not uphill to the left).

12.3 Enter boat ramp parking area.

12.4 Trail starts again across parking area (marked by red post).

12.5 Stay left at a trail junction.

13.3 Stay right at a trail junction.

13.5 After walking down a steep set of stairs, intersect with a paved road, go left.

13.7 Junction with Scoggins Valley Road; go right.

13.8 Junction with West Shore Drive, go right across the dam.

14.5 End back at parking area.

In Portland

Leif Erikson Drive
Out-and-Back

Location: North slope of Portland's west hills.

Distance: 22.6 miles (this ride can be shortened by turning around sooner).

Time: 1 to 3 hours.

Tread: 22.6 miles gravel-and-dirt road.

Season: All year; expect mud in winter and spring.

Aerobic level: Easy to moderate; expect several gradual climbs.

Technical difficulty: 1 to 2.

Hazards: The roads and firelanes are not marked very well. Lots of hikers and runners. Use caution when passing, and control your speed. Remember that all singletrack in Forest Park is closed to mountain bikes.

Highlights: This is a gated road traversing Forest Park, which is one of the largest city parks in the country. The trail is close to town, surrounded by deep forest, and has a couple of great views of the city.

•Leif Erikson Drive Out-and-Back

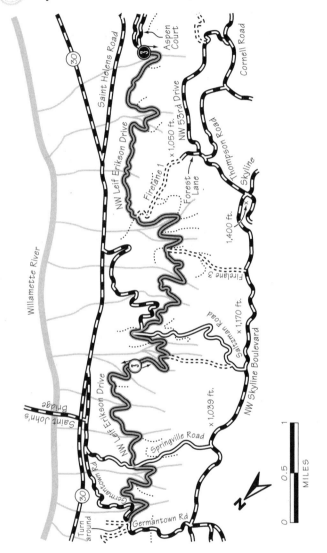

Land status: Portland City Parks.

Maps: *Mountain Biking Greater Portland*—Fat Tire Publications; USGS Portland, Linnton.

Access: Go to the end of NW Thurman Street off of NW 23rd or go to the large parking area off Germantown Road at the far end of the ride (car break-ins are not uncommon at this parking area so be sure not to leave valuables in your car).

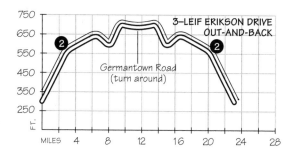

The Ride

0.0 Start at end of NW Thurman Street. (For a brisk warm-up try parking down the street and ride up the hill to the end of NW Thurman Street.) Begin gradually climbing and descending as the road goes in and out of creek drainages.

3.0 Continue straight on Leif Erikson Drive as you pass Firelane 1 on the left. This is the first of four firelanes that connect Leif Erikson Drive with Skyline Boulevard.

3.4 Notice a trail on the left, which is closed to bikes.

3.7 Gated road on the left, which is closed to bikes.

4.2 Firelane 3 on the left; continue straight.

5.2 Gated road on the left; continue straight.

6.2	Junction with Saltzman Road. This is a good turn-around point if you want a shorter ride.
9.1	Hardesty Trail on the left; continue straight.
9.4	Four-way junction with Springville Road; continue straight.
11.3	Junction with Germantown Road; turn around here.
22.6	Return to the gate at NW Thurman Street.

Firelanes 1 and 3 Loop

Location: North slope of Portland's west hills.

Distance: 10.5 miles.

Time: 1 to 2 hours.

Tread: 9.4 miles gravel firelane; 1.1 miles pavement.

Season: All year; expect mud in winter and spring.

Aerobic level: Strenuous, steep climbs.

Technical difficulty: 3; steep, slick descents.

Hazards: The roads and firelanes are not marked very well. Lots of hikers and runners. Use caution when passing, and control your speed. Remember that all singletrack in Forest Park is closed to mountain bikes.

Highlights: Utilizing Leif Erikson Drive, Firelanes 1 and 3, and Skyline Boulevard, this loop is a good training ride

•Firelanes 1 and 3 Loop

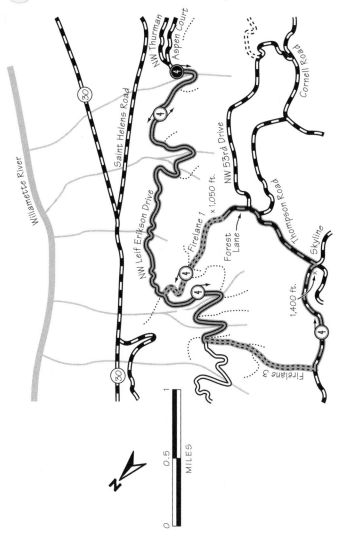

within city limits. Expect fast downhills, steep climbs, and some good cruising terrain.

Land status: Portland City Parks.

Maps: *Mountain Biking Greater Portland*—Fat Tire Publications; USGS Portland, Linnton.

Access: Go to the end of NW Thurman Street off of NW 23rd Street.

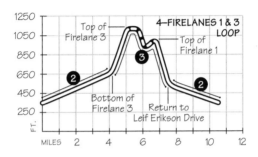

The Ride

0.0 Start at end of NW Thurman Street. (For a brisk warm-up try parking down the street and ride up the hill to the end of NW Thurman.) After rounding the gate onto Leif Erikson Drive, begin gradually climbing and descending as the road goes in and out of several creek drainages.

3.1 Continue straight on Leif Erikson Drive as you pass Firelane 1 on the left. This is the first of four firelanes that connect Leif Erikson Drive with Skyline Boulevard.

3.4 Notice a trail on the left, which is closed to bikes.

3.7 Gated road on the left, which is closed to bikes.

4.2 Look for Firelane 3 on the left; gear down and take this rougher route as it climbs steeply away from

Leif Erikson Drive. Try to settle into a rhythm because you are in for an intense mile of climbing.

4.5 Cross the Wildwood Trail and continue climbing. Note that the Wildwood Trail is closed to mountain bikes.

5.2 Round a gate and hit a junction with Skyline Boulevard, bear left on this paved road as it travels the crest of the Tualatin Mountains.

5.6 Junction with Thompson Road; head left onto Thompson Road as it drops steeply.

6.2 Bear left on NW 53rd Drive and head uphill for a short distance.

6.3 Look for Forest Lane on your left, take this gravel lane as it turns into Firelane 1 after rounding a gate. Descend gradually at first but be prepared for several long steep drops shortly.

6.9 Use caution near the intersection with the Wildwood Trail; continue descending steeply.

7.4 Junction back to Leif Erikson Drive; head right at this point back to NW Thurman Street.

10.5 Return to gate.

Long Firelane Loop

Location: North slope of Portland's west hills.

Distance: 21.2 miles.

Time: 2 to 3 hours.

Tread: 19.2 miles gravel fireroad; 2 miles pavement.

Season: All year; expect mud in winter and spring.

Aerobic level: Strenuous; steep climbs.

Technical difficulty: 3; steep, slick descents.

Hazards: The roads and firelanes are not marked very well. Lots of hikers and runners. Use caution when passing, and control your speed. Traffic on Skyline Boulevard. Remember that all singletrack in Forest Park is closed to mountain bikes.

Highlights: This is a long figure-8 loop utilizing several firelanes, Leif Erikson Drive, and Skyline Boulevard. Expect steep climbs and descents, long cruising sections, and some nice views.

Land status: Portland City Parks.

Maps: *Mountain Biking Greater Portland*—Fat Tire Publications; USGS Portland, Linnton.

Access: Go to the end of NW Thurman Street off of NW 23rd Street.

•Long Firelane Loop

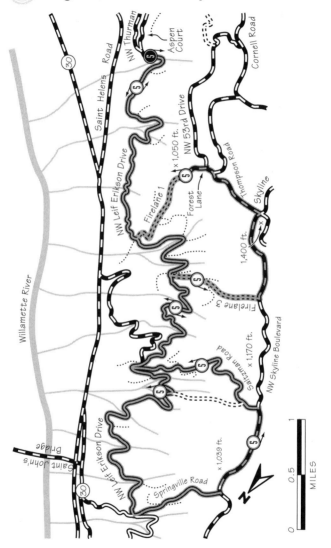

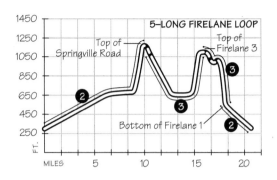

```
1450
1250                        5-LONG FIRELANE LOOP
         Top of                      Top of
1050   Springville Road            Firelane 3
 850                                        3
 650     2
 450                              3
                      Bottom of Firelane 1        2
 250
 FT.
     MILES    5        10        15        20
```

The Ride

0.0 Start at end of NW Thurman Street. (For a brisk warm-up try parking down the street and ride up the hill to the end of NW Thurman Street.) Round the gate and begin riding on Leif Erikson Drive as it rolls in and out of multiple creek drainages.

3.1 Continue straight on Leif Erikson Drive as you pass Firelane 1 on the left. This is the first of four fire-lanes that connect Leif Erikson Drive with Skyline Boulevard.

3.4 Notice a trail on the left, which is closed to bikes.

3.7 Gated road on the left, which is closed to bikes.

4.2 Firelane 3 on the left; continue straight.

5.2 Gated road on the left; continue straight.

6.2 Four-way intersection with Saltzman Road; continue straight.

9.1 Hardesty Trail on the left; continue straight.

9.5 Four-way junction with Springville Road; hang a left at this point and begin climbing steeply.

9.9 Junction with the Wildwood Trail; continue climbing uphill on Springville Road.

10.2 Hit paved Skyline Boulevard, head left, and traverse the ridgeline.

11.1 Head left on Saltzman Road and begin descending immediately.

11.3 Keep right at an intersection with another firelane and continue descending.

12.4 Cross the Wildwood Trail, but stay on Saltzman Road.

12.9 Intersect Leif Erikson Drive; head right at this point and roll along until reaching Firelane 3.

14.9 Look for Firelane 3 on the right; gear down and take this rougher route as is climbs steeply away from Leif Erikson Drive. Try to settle into a rhythm as you are in for an intense mile of climbing.

15.2 Cross the Wildwood Trail and continue climbing. Note that the Wildwood Trail is closed to mountain bikes.

15.9 Round a gate and reach a junction with Skyline Boulevard; bear left on this paved road as it travels the crest of the Tualatin Mountains.

16.3 Junction with Thompson Road; head left on Thompson Road as it drops steeply.

16.9 Bear left on NW 53rd Drive and head uphill for a short while.

17.0 Look for Forest Lane on your left, take this gravel lane as it turns into Firelane 1 after rounding a gate. Descend gradually at first but be prepared for several steep drops shortly.

17.6 Use caution near the intersection with the Wildwood Trail; continue descending steeply.

18.1 Junction back to Leif Erikson Drive, head right at this point back to NW Thurman Street.

21.2 Return to gate.

The Wildside of Forest Park

Location: North slope of Portland's west hills.

Distance: 8.1-mile loop (30.7 if riding to and from town on Leif Erikson Drive).

Time: 1.5 to 2 hours.

Tread: 7.3 miles gravel firelane; 0.8 mile pavement.

Season: All year; expect mud in winter and spring.

Aerobic level: Strenuous; steep climbs.

Technical difficulty: 3; steep, slick descents.

Hazards: The roads and firelanes are not marked very well. More remote than the other routes in Forest Park. Hikers and runners. Use caution when passing, and control your speed. Remember that all singletrack in Forest Park is closed to mountain bikes.

Highlights: Challenging descents, tough climbs, and great views.

Land status: Portland City Parks.

Maps: *Mountain Biking Greater Portland*—Fat Tire Publications; USGS Portland, Linnton.

Access: In Portland from the west end of the St. Johns Bridge, take Germantown Road 1.3 miles to a parking area on the left. Car break-ins have been a problem here, so don't leave any valuables in your car.

•The Wildside of Forest Park

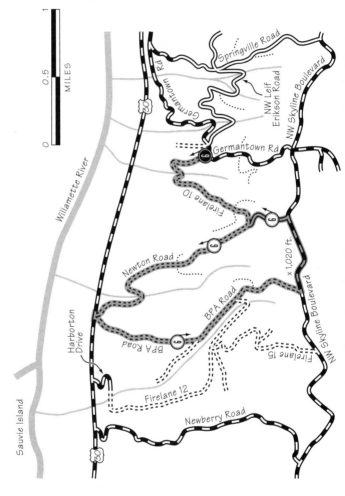

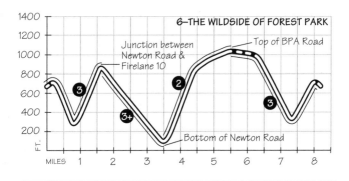

Junction between Newton Road & Firelane 10

Top of BPA Road

Bottom of Newton Road

The Ride

0.0 From the parking area ride uphill on Germantown Road.

0.1 Look for Firelane 10 on your right; go around the gate and begin descending steeply on sometimes rough terrain.

0.7 Notice a trail on your right; stay on the firelane to the left as it begins climbing steeply.

1.4 Junction with the Wildwood Trail; continue uphill on Firelane 10.

1.6 Reach a gate and parking area. Begin looking for Newton Road, which starts on the right through a gate. You will traverse on this road for a short time then descend rapidly all the way down to U.S. Highway 30 next to the Willamette River.

2.2 Cross the Wildwood Trail.

3.5 Junction with the BPA Road next to U.S. 30 near some large power lines. Head left on the rough gravel of the BPA Road, which parallels the power lines, and begin a steep, unrelenting, nearly 1,000-vertical-foot climb over the next mile.

4.5 Whew! End of the steep climbing. Intersect a doubletrack on the right; keep left and begin a long rolling section.

4.9 Junction with Firelane 12 on the right; keep straight and continue rolling along the ridgeline.

5.1 Junction with the Wildwood Trail on the left; continue along the BPA Road.

5.5 Reach Skyline Boulevard; head left on this paved road as it winds along the top of the ridgeline.

6.1 Look for Newton Road on the left; head down this gravel road to a large parking area.

6.5 At the parking area, head right and retrace the route along Firelane 10 (you will descend and then climb back up to Germantown Road).

8.0 At Germantown Road, head left downhill back to your car.

8.1 Parking area.

Note: To lengthen this ride significantly start and end the ride on Leif Erikson Drive. It will add 22.6 miles, but I've seen it done by strong riders.

Powell Butte

Location: Southeast Portland.

Distance: Varies.

Time: 1 to 2 hours.

Tread: Singletrack; gravel and pavement.

Season: All year; expect mud in winter and spring.

Aerobic level: Moderate; short, steep climbs.

Technical difficulty: 3; some rocky and slick sections.

Hazards: Lots of hikers and equestrians use this park so it's very important to control your speed and be courteous.

Highlights: Fun singletrack in the city; nice views and good exercise.

Land status: Portland City Parks.

Maps: *Mountain Biking Greater Portland*—Fat Tire Publications; USGS Gladstone.

Access: From Interstate 205 in Portland, take SE Powell Boulevard east to SE 162nd Avenue and head south to the parking area at the end of the road.

The Ride

Because Powell Butte packs so many trails in such a small area it's hard to describe any specific rides, so the best

•Powell Butte

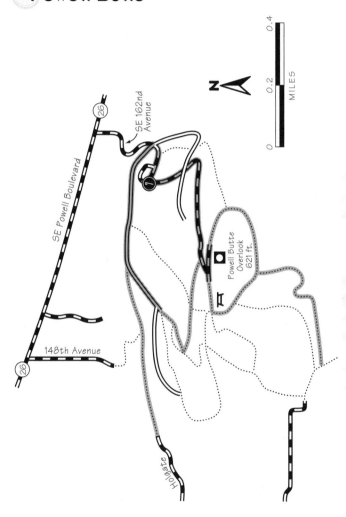

SE 162nd Avenue

SE Powell Boulevard

148th Avenue

Holgate

Powell Butte
Overlook
621 ft.

N

0   0.2   0.4
MILES

approach is to use the map with its rating symbols to pick a ride. Several trails lead toward the open summit from the parking area as well as off the back of the summit toward the Springwater Corridor. The Springwater Corridor is a paved bikeway, which cuts from near downtown through southeast Portland and into the suburbs. It's a nice alternative to driving to Powell Butte. Many of the trails on Powell Butte are closed to bikes, so please respect these closures and stick to the open routes.

Molalla River Corridor

Molalla River Corridor Trails

Location: Molalla River Corridor southeast of Portland.

Distance: Varies.

Time: 1 to 3 hours.

Tread: Singletrack; doubletrack; gravel.

Season: Summer and fall.

Aerobic level: Moderate to strenuous; short, steep climbs.

Technical difficulty: 3 to 4; lots of rocky and slick sections.

Hazards: This is a multiuse recreation area, so control your speed and be aware of other users. When conditions are muddy, trails in the Molalla River Corridor are closed.

Highlights: Lots of singletrack, some nice views, and fairly close to town.

Land status: Bureau of Land Management.

Maps: *Mountain Biking Greater Portland*—Fat Tire Publications; USGS Wilhoit, Fernwood.

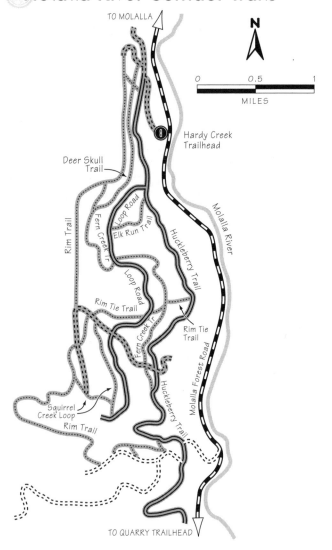

•Molalla River Corridor Trails

TO MOLALLA

N

0   0.5   1
MILES

Hardy Creek
Trailhead

Molalla River

Deer Skull
Trail

Rim Trail

Fern Creek Tr

Loop Road

Elk Run Trail

Huckleberry Trail

Loop Road

Rim Tie Trail

Fern Creek Tr

Rim Tie
Trail

Molalla Forest Road

Squirrel
Creek Loop

Rim Trail

Huckleberry Trail

TO QUARRY TRAILHEAD

Access: From Portland head south on Oregon Highway 213 for 34 miles to Molalla. From there, take Mathias, Freyer, and Dickey Prairie Roads southeast 9 miles to the Molalla Forest Road and the Hardy Creek Trailhead.

The Ride

This is another area with a large number of trails packed into a small area. Your best bet is to look at the map and put together small sections of trails to come up with a ride that suits your time and riding ability. Expect several steep sections heading up to the Rim Trail as well as some technical sections.

Mount Hood Area

Old Salmon River Trail

Location: Base of Mount Hood, east of Portland.

Distance: 5-mile loop.

Time: 1 to 2 hours.

Tread: 3.65 miles singletrack; 2.35 miles pavement.

Season: All year; expect mud in winter and spring.

Aerobic level: Easy; a couple of short steep climbs.

Technical difficulty: 2+; a couple of steep descents.

Hazards: A few sections of steep sidehill, slick bridges, and traffic on the Old Salmon River Road.

Highlights: Although this is a short loop, it has some fun singletrack and some wonderful pools along the Salmon River.

Land status: Mount Hood National Forest.

Maps: Zig Zag Ranger District map or Mount Hood National Forest Map; USGS Rhododendron.

Access: From Portland drive east on U.S. Highway 26 for approximately 42 miles. In Welches, turn right onto Old Salmon River Road (Forest Service 2618) and proceed 2.3 miles to the trailhead on your right.

•Old Salmon River Trail

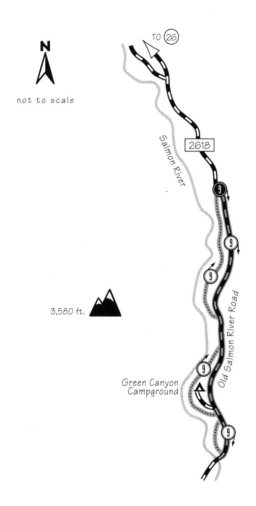

N

not to scale

TO (26)

Salmon River

2618

9

9

9

3,580 ft.

Old Salmon River Road

9

Green Canyon
Campground

9

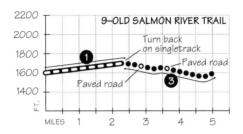

The Ride

0.0 Begin by riding up the Old Salmon River Road as it gently climbs and descends along the river. You may see the trail on your right several times along the way as it touches the road in a couple of places.

2.3 Look for the south trailhead to the Old Salmon River Trail 742A on your right just before the road crosses the Salmon River. Take this trail (it will double-back between the road and river).

2.5 The trail joins the road; follow the road briefly until the trail begins again on the left.

2.6 Trail begins again on the left; descend toward Green Canyon Campground.

2.7 Enter Green Canyon Campground; follow the trail as it winds along the river.

3.4 The trail will join the road again; follow the road until the trail starts again on the left.

3.5 Trail leaves the road on the left. Begin a section of steeper sidehill riding with some steeper climbing and descending.

4.4 Walk a section of stairs.

4.6 Begin a steep climb as the trail begins to work its way back to the road.

5.0 End the ride back at the north trailhead.

Still Creek/Pioneer Bridle Loop

Location: Base of Mount Hood near Government Camp.

Distance: 22-mile loop.

Time: 3 to 4 hours.

Tread: 9.8 miles singletrack; 11.1 miles gravel; 1.1 miles pavement.

Season: Summer and fall.

Aerobic level: Moderate; long gradual climbs.

Technical difficulty: 3+; a couple of steep, loose descents.

Hazards: Traffic on Still Creek Road, loose spots on the Pioneer Bridle Trail.

Highlights: Riding along Still Creek, the views from Trillium Lake, and the smooth singletrack on the Crosstown Trail.

Land status: Mount Hood National Forest.

Maps: *Mountain Biking Greater Portland*—Fat Tire Publications; USGS Rhododendron, Government Camp, Mount Hood South.

Access: From Portland follow U.S. Highway 26 east approximately 46 miles. Go past Welches, Rhododendron, and Zig Zag to the Camp Creek Campground on the right; park here.

•Still Creek/Pioneer Bridle Loop

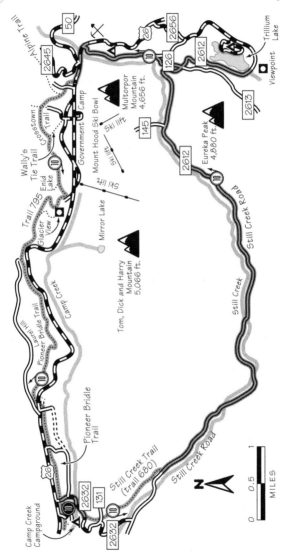

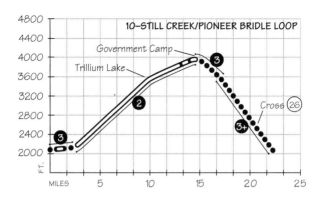

The Ride

0.0 Head out of the campground bearing east on the Pioneer Bridle Trail.

0.2 Go right on paved Forest Service 2632.

0.7 Look for the Still Creek Trail 680 on your left. Take this as it climbs and descends toward Still Creek Road.

1.0 Cross a gravel road.

1.9 Junction with the Still Creek Road. Go left on this gravel road and begin a long ascent toward Trillium Lake as the road parallels and crosses Still Creek several times.

8.0 Notice FS 145 on your left; continue straight.

9.1 Reach a four-way junction; continue straight at this point for the short out-and-back to Trillium Lake.

10.3 Reach the causeway at Trillium Lake where you can enjoy the view and take a swim. From here you will turn around and head back to the four-way intersection.

11.5   Four-way intersection; go right on FS 126.

11.9   Bear left at a junction, proceding through a large meadow and then through a Forest Service campground.

13.0   Junction with U.S. 26, bear left on the highway toward Government Camp.

13.6   As you come into Government Camp look for the Crosstown Trail on your right, next to offices for the ski hill. Climb steeply up the ski slope.

13.9   After crossing a doubletrack road, you will junction with the Alpine Trail, which comes down from the Timberline Ski Resort. Continue straight on a fun section of singletrack.

14.5   Cross the Glade Trail.

15.1   See Wally's Tie Trail on your left; continue straight.

16.1   A faint trail on the right leads to Enid Lake; continue straight on the main trail.

16.5   Glacier View Snowpark. Take the Pioneer Bridle Trail, which begins on the right where the Crosstown Trail ends.

17.2   Small trail back to the left; continue straight.

17.9   Junction with a paved road; bear left through a short tunnel.

20.5   After a short climb and a steep, loose descent the trail will come out back at U.S. 26, carefully cross at this point and pick up the trail again on the other side. The trail will descend gradually over sometimes rough terrain, crossing several gravel roads on a course that parallels U.S. 26.

21.8   Cross paved road FS 2632.

22.0   Bear left on the Camp Creek Campground access road and head back to your car.

Still Creek
Out-and-Back

Location: Base of Mount Hood near Government Camp.

Distance: 20.6 miles.

Time: 3 to 4 hours.

Tread: 2.8 miles singletrack; 16.8 miles gravel; 1 mile pavement.

Season: Summer and fall.

Aerobic level: Moderate; long gradual climbs.

Technical difficulty: 2+; a couple of narrow sections of singletrack.

Hazards: Traffic on Still Creek Road, narrow rocky spots on the Still Creek Trail 680.

Highlights: Riding along Still Creek, the views from Trillium Lake, and fun singletrack on the Still Creek Trail.

Land status: Mount Hood National Forest.

Maps: *Mountain Biking Greater Portland*—Fat Tire Publications; USGS Rhododendron, Government Camp, Mount Hood South.

Access: Follow U.S. Highway 26 approximately 46 miles due east of Portland past Welches and Rhododendron to the Camp Creek Campground on the right; park here.

•Still Creek Out-and-Back

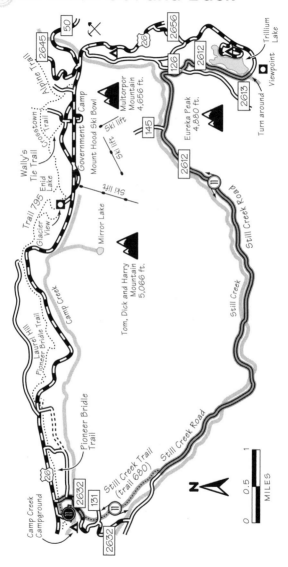

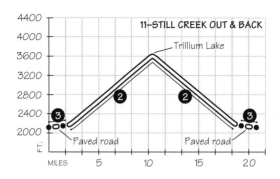

The Ride

0.0 Head out of the campground, bearing east on the Pioneer Bridle Trail.

0.2 Go right on paved Forest Service 2632.

0.7 Look for the Still Creek Trail 680 on your left; take this as it climbs and descends toward Still Creek Road.

1.0 Cross a gravel road.

1.9 Junction with Still Creek Road. Go left on this gravel road and begin a long ascent toward Trillium Lake as the road parallels and crosses Still Creek several times.

8.0 Notice FS 145 on your left and continue straight.

9.1 Reach a four-way junction; continue straight at this point for the short out-and-back to Trillium Lake.

10.3 Reach the causeway at Trillium Lake where you can enjoy the view and take a swim. From here you will turn around and retrace your route to Camp Creek Campground.

20.6 Reach Camp Creek Campground.

Barlow Road

Location: Base of Mount Hood east of Government Camp.

Distance: 17.5 miles one way with a shuttle, or 39.5 miles looping back on pavement.

Time: 3 to 4 hours.

Tread: 17.5 miles of rough doubletrack jeep road.

Season: Summer and fall.

Aerobic level: Strenuous; a couple of long, steep climbs.

Technical difficulty: 3; some steep and rough descents.

Hazards: Some loose corners; watch for occasional horses and 4-wheel-drive vehicles.

Highlights: This is the overland route of the Oregon Trail into the Willamette Valley. Interpretive signs along the way will give you a sense of what the pioneers went through at the end of their journey to Oregon. Expect some fun riding as the road descends, climbs, and then descends again. Wooden posts emblazoned with a wagon wheel logo mark the entire length of the Barlow Road.

Land status: Mount Hood National Forest.

Maps: *Mountain Biking Greater Portland*—Fat Tire Publications; USGS Mount Hood South, Badger Lake, Post Point, Rock Creek Reservoir.

Access: From Portland follow U.S. Highway 26 approximately 56 miles due east (past Government Camp) to the

•Barlow Road

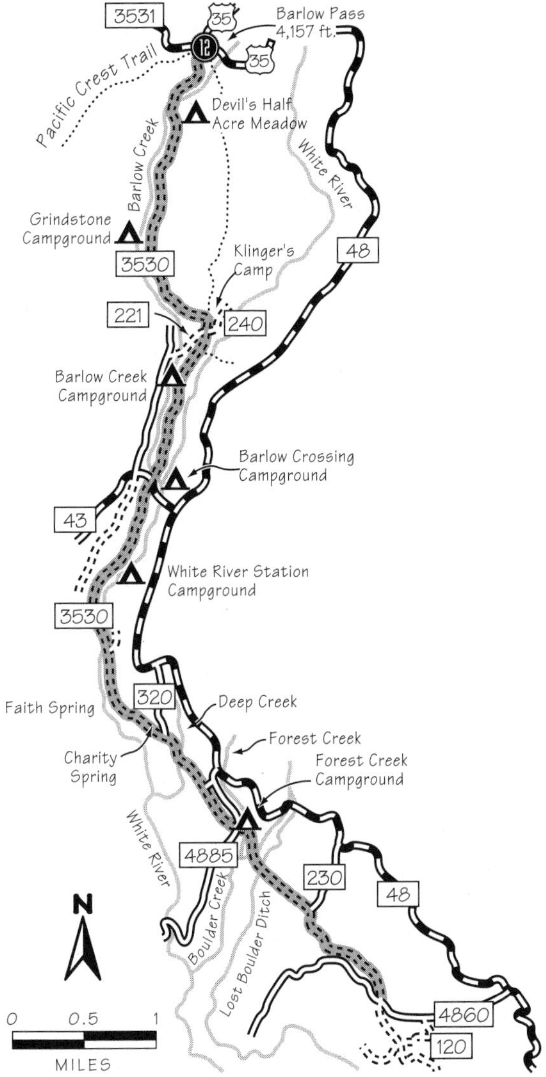

3531

Barlow Pass
4,157 ft.

35

12

35

Pacific Crest Trail

Barlow Creek

Devil's Half
Acre Meadow

White River

Grindstone
Campground

3530

Klinger's
Camp

48

221

240

Barlow Creek
Campground

Barlow Crossing
Campground

43

White River Station
Campground

3530

Faith Spring

320

Deep Creek

Charity
Spring

Forest Creek

Forest Creek
Campground

White River

4885

230

48

N

Boulder Creek

Lost Boulder Ditch

4860

120

0   0.5   1

MILES

junction with U.S. 35. Take U.S. 35 north 2 miles to Barlow Pass. The access road to the trailhead is on the right; follow it around the corner to a large parking area.

If shuttling this ride you will want to first leave a car at the end of the ride, near the junction of Forest Service 4860 and Forest Service 3530.

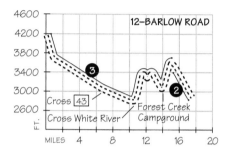

The Ride

0.0 Look for the beginning of the Barlow Road at the near end of the parking area. The riding begins fast and furious as the road descends aggressively for the first mile. (Note that several trails converge at this trailhead; be sure to start on the actual Barlow Road as it heads southeast from Barlow Pass.)

1.0 As the road begins to level out you will come into the Devil's Half Acre Meadow and Devil's Half Acre Campground on the left. Notice the first of several interpretive signs.

3.2 After several seasonally wet crossings, the road rolls along through dense old-growth forest to the Grindstone Campground on the right.

4.9 After another section of rolling terrain, which can be rough at times, you'll come to the Klinger's Camp interpretive site.

5.0 Junction with FS 240 on the left and FS 221 on the right; continue straight.

5.3 Trail junction on the left; continue straight.

5.5 Access road to Barlow Creek Campground on the right; continue straight as the road descends on a sandy surface.

7.3 After paralleling Barlow Creek, you'll see Barlow Crossing Campground on the left. Continue straight as the road crosses over Barlow Creek.

7.4 Junction with paved road FS 43; cross over and continue along the Barlow Road as it traverses an old floodplain.

8.6 Look for White River Station Campground on the left. Begin a short climb.

10.0 Descend to the White River. Notice the murky color of the river, which comes directly from the White River Glacier on Mount Hood. After crossing the river the road briefly follows its course.

10.5 Begin a steep climb as the road leaves the river at a dispersed campsite. Notice several springs as you negotiate this lung- and thigh-busting climb.

11.7 Junction with road FS 270 at the top of the climb; continue straight as the road descends and climbs steeply.

12.7 Reach a junction with gravel road FS 011 on the left, with a sign denoting a vehicle detour. You can continue straight, through a barrier.

13.6 Cross a gravel road and proceed past Forest Creek Campground on the left as the road descends to a bridge over Boulder Creek. After crossing the creek begin another long steep climb.

15.2 Top of climb. Whew!

15.6 Junction with gravel road FS 230 on the left, proceed straight as the road begins descending again.

17.5 Junction with gravel road FS 4860; end the ride here at your shuttle car or head left toward FS 48 and the long climb back to the top.

Note: For the optional loop ride, head left on FS 4860 and then take another left onto FS 48, a paved road. Follow FS 48 all the way to U.S. Highway 35, where you turn left toward Barlow Pass and your car.

Bennett Pass Road Out-and-Back

Location: Base of Mount Hood east of Government Camp.

Distance: 23.6 miles.

Time: 3 to 4 hours.

Tread: 23.6 miles gravel jeep road.

Season: Midsummer through fall.

Aerobic level: Strenuous; a couple of long steep climbs.

Technical difficulty: 3; some steep and rough sections.

Hazards: Some fast, rocky descents with lots of shaded areas and exposure.

•Bennett Pass Road Out-and-Back

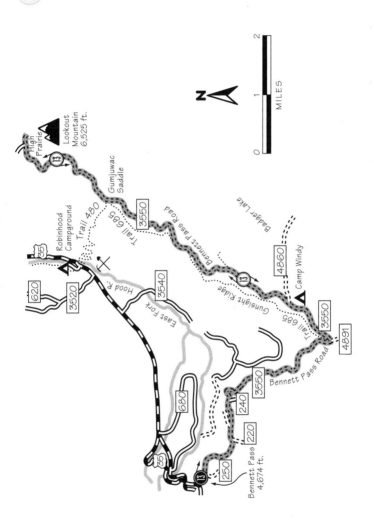

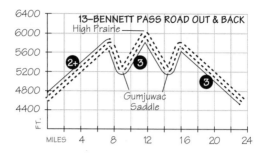

Highlights: A very scenic out-and-back ride, with close-up views of Mount Hood as well as views into the Badger Creek Wilderness. Expect some tough climbing and fun descents. Try the hike up to Lookout Mountain for an even better view.

Land status: Mount Hood National Forest.

Maps: *Mountain Biking Greater Portland*—Fat Tire Publications; USGS Mount Hood South, Badger Lake.

Access: From Portland, follow U.S. Highway 26 approximately 56 miles due east (past Government Camp) to the junction with U.S. 35. Take U.S. 35 north 7 miles to Bennett Pass; Bennett Pass Road is on the right, just past the exit to Mount Hood Meadows Ski Area. Follow it around the corner to a large parking area.

The Ride

0.0 Begin by climbing up the well graded Bennett Pass Road (Forest Service 3550) as it climbs gently toward Gunsight Ridge.

1.2 The road forks, stay to the right on FS 3550. Shortly thereafter begin climbing more steeply as the road becomes rougher.

2.5 Thread the needle as the road traverses a sheer cliff.

3.1 Negotiate a rough section as the road crosses a steep scree slope.

4.2 Junction with the Bonney Meadows Road (FS 4891); bear left and begin a series of climbs and descents as you ride below the crest of Gunsight Ridge. Notice a trail on your left just before the junction. This is the Gunsight Ridge Trail 685, which parallels the road you will be riding.

5.2 Junction with FS 4860 at Camp Windy; continue straight. Camp Windy is a relatively unimproved campground in a meadow area with several small springs. Here the road becomes rougher with several rutted sections as it rolls along the ridge.

6.7 Notice Jean Lake Trail on your right; this trail is not open to bikes but it is a nice short hike to Jean Lake.

7.2 Gunsight Ridge Trail enters the road on the left.

7.4 Begin a short climb as the road opens up to a viewpoint.

7.8 Begin a fun descent toward Gumjuwac Saddle.

8.9 Reach Gumjuwac Saddle; several trails converge at this point. Those to the east enter the Badger Creek Wilderness. Continue straight on FS 3550 as it climbs easily to a spectacular viewpoint of Mount Hood.

10.0 Reach the viewpoint. From here the road climbs 800 feet over the next 1.8 miles to High Prairie, so feel free to turn around or continue on to even better views and a nice hike up Lookout Mountain.

11.8 High Prairie; turn around and retrace your route. If you're feeling up to it, be sure to hike up Lookout Mountain.

23.6 End back at the parking area.

Gunsight/Gumjuwac
Loop

Location: Base of Mount Hood east of Government Camp.

Distance: 16.2-mile loop.

Time: 3 to 4 hours.

Tread: 7.5 miles singletrack; 4.4 miles gravel jeep road; 4.3 miles pavement.

Season: Midsummer through fall.

Aerobic level: Strenuous; a couple of long steep climbs.

Technical difficulty: 4; rocky singletrack, steep descents, and switchbacks.

Hazards: Switchbacks will sneak up on you; narrow trail, rocks, and long steep descent.

Highlights: A very scenic loop ride and an aerobic workout for strong riders; great views of Mount Hood; technical singletrack and an aerobic workout.

Land status: Mount Hood National Forest.

Maps: *Mountain Biking Greater Portland*—Fat Tire Publications; USGS Mount Hood South, Badger Lake.

Access: From Portland follow U.S. Highway 26 approximately 56 miles due east (past Government Camp) to the junction with U.S. 35. Take U.S. 35 north 11.3 miles to the Gumjuwac Trailhead. The Gumjuwac Trailhead parking

•Gunsight/Gumjuwac Loop

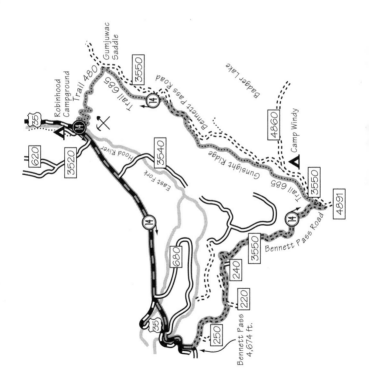

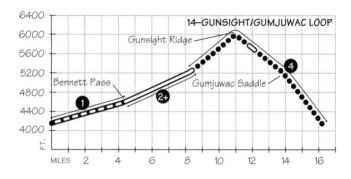

area is on the east side of the highway opposite Robinhood Campground. Park here.

The Ride

0.0 Begin by riding back up U.S. 35 for 4.3 miles to Bennett Pass.

4.3 At Bennett Pass head left on well-graded Bennett Pass Road (Forest Service 3550) as it climbs toward Gunsight Ridge.

5.5 The road forks. Stay to the right on FS 3550, shortly thereafter begin climbing more steeply as the road becomes rougher.

6.8 Thread the needle as the road traverses a shear cliff.

7.4 Negotiate a rough section as the road crosses a steep scree slope.

8.5 Just before the junction with the Bonney Meadows Road (FS 4891), take a left on Gunsight Ridge Trail 685. Begin climbing steeply as the trail reaches the ridgeline and begins rolling along it.

11.1 Reach a viewpoint. Take a minute to walk out to this scenic spot high above the valley below. The trail descends steeply to FS 3550.

11.5	The trail touches the road.
11.8	The trail joins FS 3550 briefly; follow it to the left for 0.2 mile.
12.0	Look for the trail as it leaves the road, then begin another series of steep climbs followed by a steep descent.
13.7	Reach Gumjuwac Saddle. Several trails meet FS 3550 at this point. Check your brakepads before you follow Trail 480 to the left (west) as it begins a long, steep descent back toward the trailhead.
14.2	Begin a series of tight switchbacks. Use caution as the trail becomes rocky with some steep dropoffs in this area. The trail continues to descend steadily with widely spaced switchbacks.
16.2	End of ride at Gumjuwac Trailhead.

Umbrella Falls/
Sahalie Falls Loop

Location: Base of Mount Hood east of Government Camp.

Distance: 5 miles.

Time: 1 to 2 hours.

Tread: 5 miles of singletrack.

Season: Midsummer through fall.

•Umbrella Falls/Sahalie Falls Loop

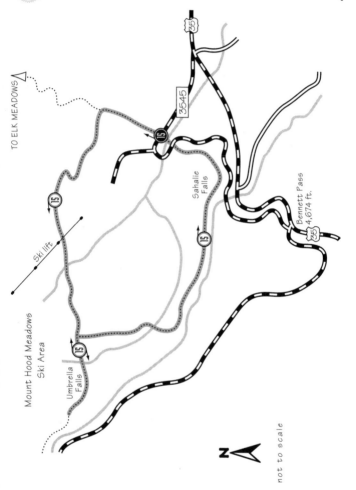

TO ELK MEADOWS

35

3545

15

Sahalie
Falls

Bennett Pass
4,674 ft.

35

15

Ski lift

15

Mount Hood Meadows
Ski Area

Umbrella
Falls

15

N

not to scale

Aerobic level: Strenuous; short, steep climbs.

Technical difficulty: 4; tight, rocky singletrack.

Hazards: Use caution near Sahalie Falls.

Highlights: This short but scenic loop can be combined with the Gunsight/Gumjuwac Loop for a very hard day of riding.

Land status: Mount Hood National Forest.

Maps: *Mountain Biking Greater Portland*—Fat Tire Publications; USGS Mount Hood South.

Access: From Portland follow U.S. Highway 26 approximately 56 miles due east (past Government Camp) to the junction with U.S. 35. Take U.S. 35 north for 8.3 miles to the turn for the Mount Hood Meadows Nordic Area on the left; follow it to the trailhead.

The Ride

0.0 Begin by riding up toward Elk Meadows.
0.4 Go left at a trail junction; do not continue toward Elk Meadows. Begin a steep climb through the Mount Hood Meadows Ski Area.

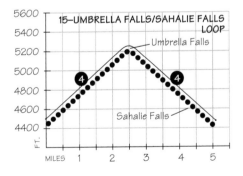

2.3 Trail junction to Umbrella Falls; continue straight (right fork) to Umbrella Falls.

2.7 Reach Umbrella Falls; after taking a break head back to the last junction.

3.1 Return to junction; head right toward Sahalie Falls on a fast downhill section.

4.4 Reach Sahalie Falls.

4.9 Junction with paved ski area access road. Cross the road and continue on the trail another 0.1 mile to your car.

5.0 End of ride.

Vancouver Area

Larch Mountain Loop

Location: East of Vancouver.

Distance: 13 miles.

Time: 2 to 3.5 hours.

Tread: 4.4 miles singletrack; 8.6 miles gravel.

Season: Late spring through fall.

Aerobic level: Strenuous; long, steep climbs.

Technical difficulty: 4+; due to the top portion of single-track.

Hazards: Rocky scree slope near the top of Larch Mountain; rock and root-strewn descent. New water bars can be extremely slick as can the several small bridges.

Highlights: If you're up to the climb and technical descents, this is a wonderful loop. The views from Larch Mountain are sweeping and the singletrack will test you.

Land status: Washington State Department of Natural Resources.

Maps: *Mountain Biking Southwest Washington*—Fat Tire Publications; USGS Dole, Larch Mountain.

Access: From Portland follow Interstate 5 north for 9 miles to Washington Highway 502 east. Follow WA 502 east for 7 miles to WA 503, and then head north on WA 503 for 6 miles to Northeast Rock Creek Road on the right. Follow this east for 8 miles to Sunset Falls Road. Go east 2 miles on Sunset Falls Road to Dole Valley Road. Follow this south 5 miles to Rock Creek Campground (45 minutes from Portland).

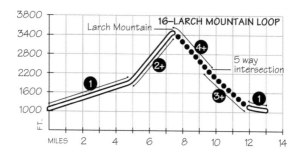

The Ride

0.0 Head out of Rock Creek Campground and go left on 1000.

0.2 Junction with 1000; stay right and begin climbing gently.

0.8 Notice 1300 on the right; continue straight.

1.2 Cross Cold Creek. Notice the singletrack trail crossing at this point; you will be coming down the trail on the left. Continue climbing.

2.4 Junction with the Larch Corrections Center access road. Keep left at this point and continue climbing.

•Larch Mountain Loop

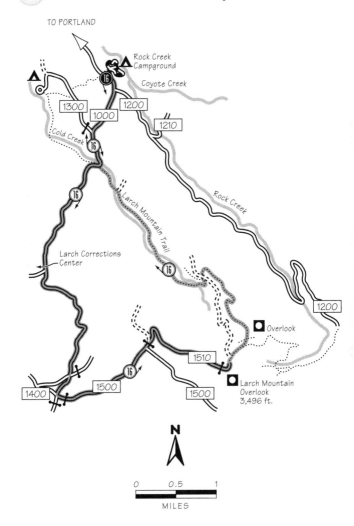

4.6 Shortly after crossing another gravel road, bear left at a four-way intersection onto 1500. Begin climbing steeply.

5.9 Bear left on 1510 through a gate, and continue climbing even more steeply.

7.4 Reach the summit of Larch Mountain and take some time to regain your breath and enjoy the view before beginning the very technical descent. Look for the trail that begins just beyond the radio facilities.

7.7 Trail junction. Head left and immediately cross another trail. Begin traversing the open scree slope. After the scree slope you will enter a long, steep section with multiple drops and rocky areas; use caution.

9.6 Reach a five-way intersection; take the second option from the left, which is basically straight downhill as it descends to Cold Creek.

10.0 Cross bridge over Cold Creek.

10.9 After several more small bridges, you will see a faint doubletrack on the right, but stay left on the trail as it parallels Cold Creek.

11.0 Cross Cold Creek again.

11.8 Reach road 1000 again and head right back toward your car.

12.8 Keep left at the junction with 1200.

13.0 Turn right into Rock Creek Campground.

Tarbell Trail Loop

Location: East of Vancouver.

Distance: 21.5 miles.

Time: 3 to 4 hours.

Tread: 10.9 miles singletrack; 10.6 miles gravel.

Season: Late spring through fall.

Aerobic level: Strenuous; long, steep climbs.

Technical difficulty: 3; several switchbacks and narrow sections of trail.

Hazards: Be aware that this trail is used frequently by equestrians, some of the switchbacks are tricky.

Highlights: A long gravel climb is rewarded by buffed-out singletrack through a second-growth forest and several nice views.

Land status: Washington State Department of Natural Resources.

Maps: *Mountain Biking Southwest Washington*—Fat Tire Publications; USGS Dole, Larch Mountain.

Access: From Portland, follow Interstate 5 north for 9 miles to Washington Highway 502 east. Follow WA 502 east for 7 miles to WA 503, and then head north on WA 503 for 6 miles to Northeast Rock Creek Road on the right. Follow this east for 8 miles to Sunset Falls Road. Go east 2 miles on Sunset Falls Road to Dole Valley Road. Follow this

Tarbell Trail Loop

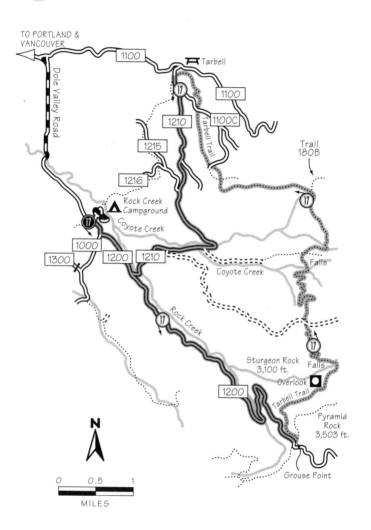

TO PORTLAND &
VANCOUVER

Dole Valley Road

1100

Tarbell

17

1100

1210

1100C

Tarbell Trail

1215

Trail
180B

1216

17

Rock Creek
Campground

Coyote Creek

17

1000

1300

1200

1210

Falls

Coyote Creek

Rock Creek

17

17

Falls

Sturgeon Rock
3,100 ft.

Overlook

Tarbell Trail

1200

Pyramid
Rock
3,503 ft.

Grouse Point

N

0   0.5   1

MILES

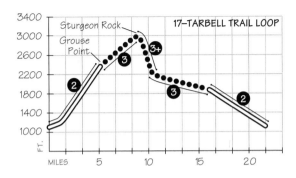

south for 5 miles to Rock Creek Campground (45 minutes from Portland).

The Ride

0.0   Head out of Rock Creek Campground and go left on L1000.

0.2   Go left on 1200 as it travels above Rock Creek.

0.9   Continue straight at the junction with L1210 and begin climbing uphill. You will return to this junction on 1210 near the end of the loop.

3.9   Cross Rock Creek and begin climbing more steeply.

5.5   The saddle at Grouse Point, where several trails junction. Head left on Tarbell Trail as it continues climbing.

5.6   Trail forks; stay left. The right trail heads up very steeply to Pyramid Rock. Begin traversing underneath Pyramid Rock.

7.3   Pass by the first of two waterfalls on this trail. Begin a section of steep climbing and switchbacks.

8.7   Cross a remote doubletrack and begin a long descent with multiple switchbacks.

10.6   Cross a singletrack.

10.8	Hidden Falls; take some time to enjoy this shaded grotto. Afterward, begin climbing steeply through a series of switchbacks.
12.5	Junction with the Chinook Trail 180B; stay left as the trail traverses below Squaw Butte.
14.3	Cross singletrack and begin descending.
14.5	Cross gravel road and continue descending.
15.6	Cross gravel road 1100C.
16.2	Trail splits; bear left down to 1210.
16.4	Junction with 1210; head left on the gravel road. Continue on this main road past several spur roads as it descends gradually back toward road 1200.
20.6	Return to the junction with 1200; head right.
21.3	Junction with 1000; head right.
21.5	Head right into Rock Creek Campground.

Three Corner Rock

Location: Washougal River drainage, east of Vancouver.

Distance: 16.6-mile loop.

Time: 3 to 4 hours.

Road: 7 miles singletrack; 9.6 miles gravel.

Season: Late spring through fall.

Technic level: Strenuous; long, steep climbs and short, climbs.

•Three Corner Rock

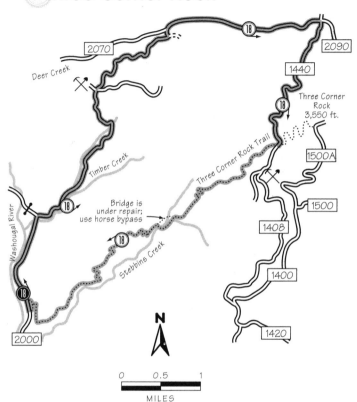

Technical difficulty: 3+; multiple switchbacks; rocky and narrow sections of trail.

Hazards: Be aware that this trail is used frequently by equestrians; some of the switchbacks are tricky.

Highlights: This loop will challenge your conditioning with short, intense singletrack climbs; long, steep gravel climbs and multiple switchbacks. But it will reward you with nice views and well-maintained singletrack.

Land status: Washington State Department of Natural Resources.

Maps: *Mountain Biking Southwest Washington*—Fat Tire Publications; USGS Bobs Mountain, Beacon Rock.

Access: From Interstate 5 in Vancouver head 16 miles east on U.S. Highway 14 to Washougal. Turn left onto 15th Street and go to Washougal River Road (Forest Service 2000). Follow Washougal River Road about 21.5 miles to the Three Corner Rock Trailhead (1 hour from Portland).

The Ride

0.0 After parking at the Three Corner Rock Trailhead, head upstream on 2000.

1.0 Immediately after crossing Timber Creek stay right at a road junction.

3.6 Reach a four-way road junction at a saddle; continue straight and begin descending.

4.9 Junction with 2070; head right and begin climbing gradually along Deer Creek.

6.9 Reach a four-way intersection; head right on gravel road 1440. Begin climbing and then descend toward the Three Corner Rock Trail.

9.4 Immediately after crossing a creek look for the trail

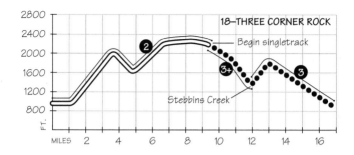

on your right; take this as it begins descending down to a ridgeline. (You may see a trail coming down on the left side of the road; this heads up to the actual Three Corner Rock but it is too steep for biking.)

10.7 Leave the ridge and begin a series of steep switchbacks.

11.8 Bear left on a faint horse trail just before the old bridge. The bridge is being rebuilt so you'll need to ford Stebbins Creek for the time being.

12.1 Rejoin the main trail, head left, and begin a steep climb through a series of switchbacks.

16.4 After a long descent, head right on gravel road 2000.

16.6 Return to trailhead.

Mount St. Helens

Old Man Pass Loop

Location: Wind River Recreation Area.

Distance: 12.7 miles.

Time: 2 to 3 hours.

Tread: 2.7 miles singletrack; 9.8 miles gravel; 0.1 mile doubletrack; 0.1 mile pavement.

Season: Late spring through fall.

Aerobic level: Moderate.

Technical difficulty: 2+.

Hazards: Trails are not well marked and can be poorly defined.

Highlights: The Forest Service has determined this area, a nordic skiing area in the winter, to be conducive to mountain biking as well. The terrain is rolling with a combination of old-growth and cleared forest, which makes for nice views and easier riding. The best aspect of this area is that very few other user groups utilize the trails in the summer, so you can expect to not see many other people.

Land status: Gifford Pinchot National Forest—Wind River Ranger District.

•Old Man Pass Loop

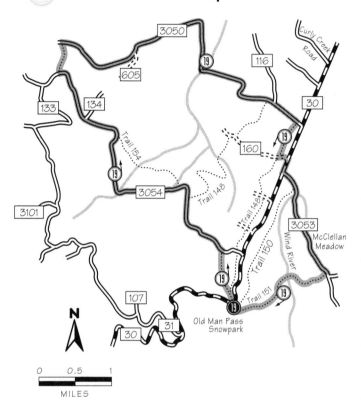

Maps: *Mountain Biking Southwest Washington*—Fat Tire Publications; USGS Termination Point, Burnt Peak.

Access: From Vancouver take U.S. Highway 14 east 49 miles to the turn for Carson on the left. Head 14 miles north on Forest Service 30 through Carson to a fork; continue right up FS 30 for 12 miles to Old Man Pass Snowpark on your left; park here (1.5 hours from Portland).

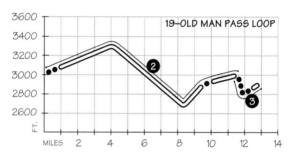

The Ride

0.0 From the parking area, find the trail beginning behind the outhouses; follow this trail as it makes its way to through the forest (be sure not to take the trail to the right).

0.6 Junction with gravel road Forest Service 3054, head left on this well-graded road as it rises and falls gently through a mixed forest.

1.6 Notice a trail leaving the road on your right. This is one of many cross-country skiing trails being converted to dual use. Continue straight on FS 3054.

4.0 Notice FS 134 on your right; continue straight on FS 3054.

4.6 Look for a faint singletrack trail on your right. You will want to take this trail as it descends gently to FS 3050.

5.0 Junction with FS 3050; head right as the gravel road continues to descend gently.

6.0 Notice FS 605 on your right; continue straight.

9.1 Notice Trail 148 coming in on your right; continue straight.

9.5 Take the return loop of Trail 148 on your right.

9.9 Junction with doubletrack FS 160; head left on this road for a short distance to paved road FS 30.

10.0 Junction with FS 30; head right.

10.1 Look for FS 3053 on your left; take this gravel road.

10.3 Notice Trail 150 on your right just before crossing Wind River; continue straight on FS 3053 (or head down Trail 150 1.3 miles to shorten the ride).

11.3 Just before crossing the end of McClellan Meadow, look for Trail 151 on your right, take this trail as it descends toward Wind River.

12.6 The trail ends at a gravel road. Take this road a short distance back to FS 30 and Old Man Pass Snowpark.

12.7 End of ride at Old Man Pass Snowpark.

Lone Butte Loop

Location: Wind River Recreation Area.

Distance: 11.7 miles.

Time: 1.5 to 2 hours.

Tread: 10.3 miles gravel; 1.4 miles doubletrack.

Season: Late spring through fall.

Aerobic level: Moderate.

Technical difficulty: 2.

Hazards: No real hazards, but be aware of traffic on Forest Service 30.

Highlights: Half of this ride follows a large meadow on a gated road, so the chances of seeing wildlife are good.

Land status: Gifford Pinchot National Forest—Wind River Ranger District.

Maps: *Mountain Biking Southwest Washington*—Fat Tire Publications; USGS Lone Butte.

Access: From Vancouver take U.S. Highway 14 east for 49 miles to the turn for Carson on the left. Head north for 14 miles on Forest Service 30 through Carson to a fork; continue right up FS 30 for 17 miles to Lone Butte Snowpark on your left; park here (1.5 hours from Portland).

•Lone Butte Loop

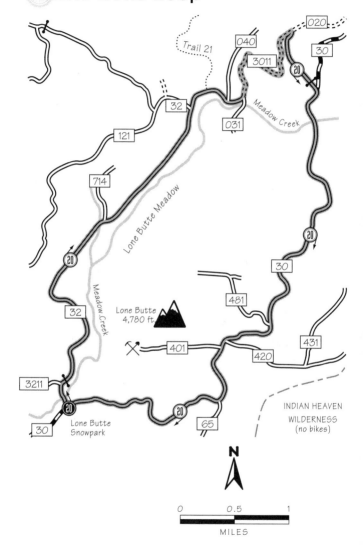

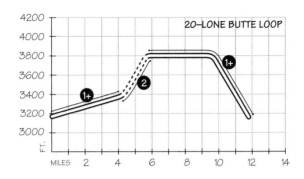

The Ride

0.0 Head out of the snowpark and immediately turn left on gravel road FS 32.

0.2 After crossing Meadow Creek, take a right on FS 32 and proceed around the gate. Begin climbing gradually above the creek.

2.2 Look for FS 714 on your left; continue straight on FS 32. Take time to check the meadow for wildlife along this section.

3.5 Road junction; FS 32 heads off to the left but you will want to continue straight on FS 3011.

3.7 Notice the trailhead for Trail 21 on the left, continue straight on FS 3011 as it begins to climb more steeply.

4.0 Continue straight at the junction with FS 040.

4.2 Bear left at the junction with FS 031 and begin climbing more steeply; the road eventually turns from gravel to dirt doubletrack.

5.6 Junction with doubletrack FS 020; head right toward FS 30.

6.2 Meet FS 30 and follow this gravel road as it traverses and then descends back to Lone Butte Snowpark.

8.8 Notice FS 481 on your right; continue straight.

9.3 Remain on FS 30 past the junctions with FS 420 and FS 401, begin descending more steeply.

10.0 Pass FS 65 on your left.

11.7 Return to Lone Butte Snowpark.

Siouxan Creek
Out-and-Back

Location: Lewis River Drainage.

Distance: 12.5 miles.

Time: 2 to 3 hours.

Tread: 12.5 miles singletrack.

Season: Late spring through fall.

Aerobic level: Moderate.

Technical difficulty: 3.

Hazards: Some exposure as the trail travels above several cliffs; several rocky areas; lots of hikers and horses on weekends.

Highlights: Amazing singletrack along a beautiful creek. You will ride above and then along Siouxan Creek with a side trip to Chinook Falls.

•Siouxan Creek Out-and-Back

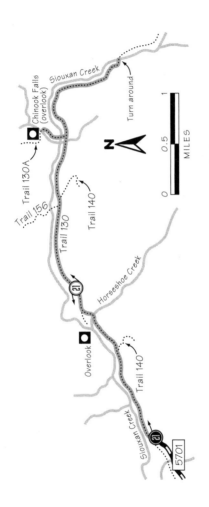

Land status: Gifford Pinchot National Forest—Wind River Ranger District.

Maps: *Mountain Biking Southwest Washington*—Fat Tire Publications; USGS Yale Dam, Siouxan Peak.

Access: From Portland, take Interstate 5 north 9 miles to Washington Highway 502. Go east on WA 502 for 7 miles to WA 503, and then head north on WA 503 for 17 miles to Forest Service 54. At the Chelatchie Prairie Store, take FS 54 east 8 miles to FS 5701 and go left. Turn left again on FS 5701 at the junction with FS 57 and continue 4 miles to the end of the road (1 hour and 15 minutes from Portland).

The Ride

0.0 From the parking area, find the access trail as it descends towards the creek. When you hit the main trail go right and begin descending down a steeper slope.

1.1 Look for Trail 140 on the right; continue straight as the trail rolls along above Siouxan Creek.

1.7 Just after crossing Horseshoe Creek, look for a trail on the left that cuts back to a viewpoint over Horseshoe Creek Falls. After checking out the view continue on the main trail.

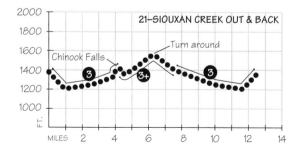

3.2	Look for Trail 156 on your left and then the return loop of Trail 140 on your right immediately after; continue straight on Trail 130.
4.0	Follow Trail 130A on the left as it crosses Siouxan Creek and then ascends toward Chinook Falls.
4.25	Chinook Falls. After viewing the falls return to the main trail.
4.5	Continue upstream on Trail 130 as it climbs and descends more steeply. Be aware that the trail becomes more exposed through this section.
6.5	Trail fords Siouxan Creek. Turn around at this point and retrace your route back to the trailhead.
12.5	Return to trailhead.

Lewis River Trail Out-and-Back

Location: Lewis River Drainage.

Distance: 19.2 miles.

Time: 3 to 4 hours.

Tread: 19.2 miles singletrack.

Season: Late spring through fall.

Aerobic level: Moderate to strenuous; several short, steep climbs.

•Lewis River Trail Out-and-Back

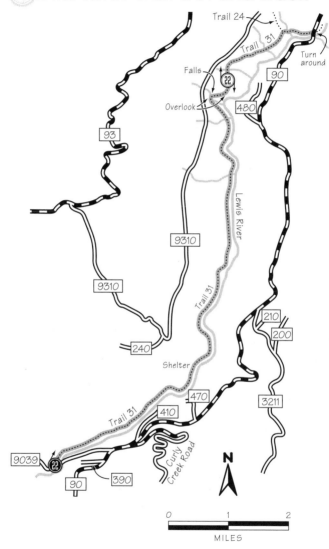

Technical difficulty: 3+.

Hazards: Exposure as the trail travels very near large cliffs; several rocky areas and a rough section over a recent landslide.

Highlights: Amazing singletrack along a beautiful river. This trail has it all, from cruising singletrack to steep climbs to a creek crossing and nice views. It's best to do this ride midweek because it is very popular on weekends with hikers.

Land status: Gifford Pinchot National Forest—Wind River Ranger District.

Maps: *Mountain Biking Southwest Washington*—Fat Tire Publications; USGS Burnt Peak, Spencer Butte.

Access: From Portland take Interstate 5 north 21 miles to Washington Highway 503. Head east on WA 503 (which turns into Forest Service 90 east of Cougar) for 52.3 miles to FS 9039 on the left, then take FS 9039 0.8 mile to the trailhead on the left just before crossing the river (1.5 to 2 hours from Portland).

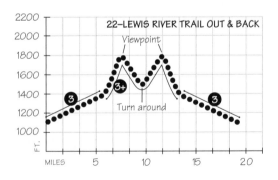

The Ride

0.0 From the parking area, cross Lewis River and immediately pick up the trail, which begins on the right. The first few miles are relatively easy with little elevation gain and few obstructions.

2.4 Look for a shelter on the left; continue as the trail rolls along the river and starts becoming more technical in places.

3.3 Enter a large slide zone. The trail has been rebuilt but is still rough in places.

7.2 After a very steep climb, cross a small creek as it drops over a rather impressive waterfall.

7.5 Use caution in this area because the trail travels very near the edge of a large cliff. Take some time to enjoy the view of the river hundreds of feet below.

8.9 Keep right at the junction with Trail 24.

9.2 After a steep descent, cross Cussed Hollow Creek, then climb steeply again before descending back to FS 90.

9.6 Reach paved road FS 90, return at this point back toward your car (or loop back the 9.3 miles on FS 90 and FS 9039).

19.2 Return to trailhead.

Ape Canyon/Plains of Abraham Out-and-Back

Location: Slopes of Mount St. Helens.

Distance: 23 miles.

Time: 3 to 5 hours.

Tread: 18.8 miles singletrack; 4.2 miles doubletrack.

Season: Summer and fall.

Aerobic level: Strenuous.

Technical difficulty: 3+.

Hazards: Exposure as the trail travels very near some large cliffs; riding along a knife-edged ridge; a couple of stair sections that require walking your bike.

Highlights: Riding on the flanks of a recently active volcano. Much of this ride is on open slopes with great views of the mountain and surrounding vistas. If you make it all the way to Windy Ridge Viewpoint be sure to check out Spirit Lake far below.

Land status: Gifford Pinchot National Forest—Mount St. Helens National Volcanic Monument.

Maps: *Mountain Biking Southwest Washington*—Fat Tire Publications; USGS Mount St. Helens, Spirit Lake West, Spirit Lake East, Smith Peak Butte.

•Ape Canyon/Plains of Abraham Out-and-Back

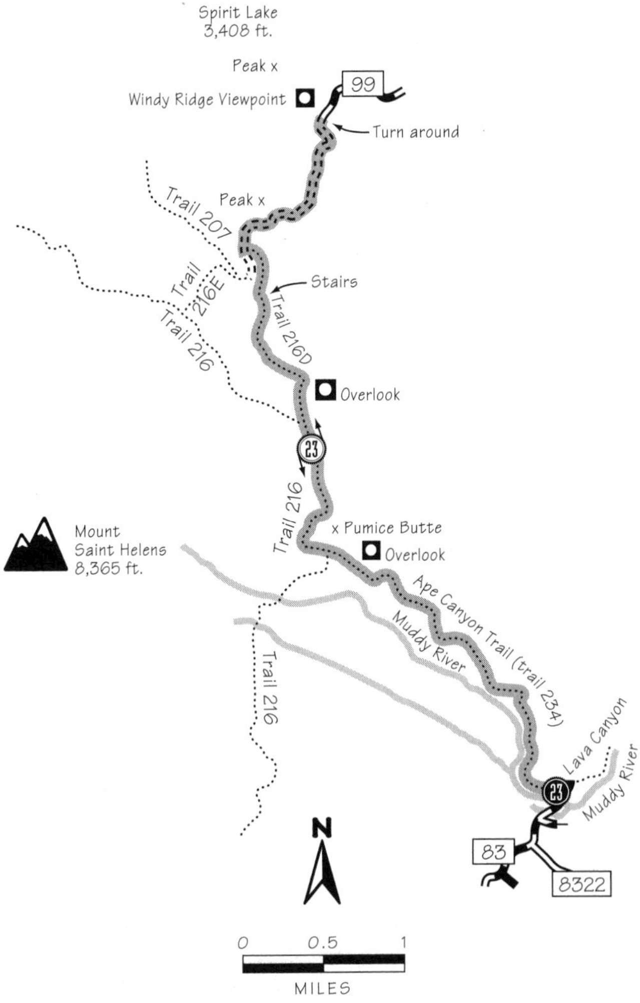

Spirit Lake
3,408 ft.

Peak x

Windy Ridge Viewpoint

99

Turn around

Peak x

Trail 207

Trail 216E

Trail 216

Stairs

Trail 216D

Overlook

23

Trail 216

x Pumice Butte

Overlook

Mount
Saint Helens
8,365 ft.

Ape Canyon Trail (trail 234)

Muddy River

Trail 216

Muddy River

Lava Canyon

23

Muddy River

83

8322

N

| 0 | 0.5 | 1 |

MILES

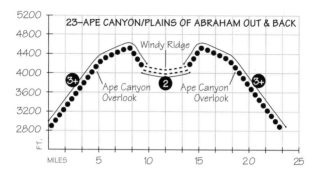

23–APE CANYON/PLAINS OF ABRAHAM OUT & BACK

Access: From Portland take Interstate 5 north 21 miles from the Columbia River Bridge to Washington Highway 503. Go east on WA 503 for 34 miles to the junction with Forest Service 83, then head north on FS 83 for 11 miles to the Ape Canyon Trailhead (1.5 to 2 hours from Portland).

The Ride

0.0 From the Ape Canyon Trailhead begin riding up Trail 234, which climbs very steeply at first over loose soil.

0.7 Begin climbing more steeply. For the next couple of miles you climb on a switchback-studded trail through a forest of large trees, which were spared destruction in the 1980 eruption.

3.5 The trail levels somewhat at this point but continues climbing along a ridge with nice views on either side.

4.9 Use caution when Ape Canyon appears on your right because the trail circles above the head of this dramatic canyon. Notice the erosion that took place as the snowmelt from the eruption careened down the mountain.

5.3	Junction with the Loowit Trail 216; head right on this trail toward the Plains of Abraham and Windy Ridge. After a short, steep climb the trail will cross several small creek drainages and then begin to level out on the broad sweep of the Plains of Abraham.
7.2	Keep right at a trail junction. Soon the trail will begin looping in and out of several creek drainages until spitting you out at the top of a knife-edged ridge.
8.5	Top of ridge; carefully make your way down toward a series of steps.
8.8	Top of a series of steps put in to control erosion down a steep slope.
9.4	Junction with doubletrack; head right toward Windy Ridge as the road climbs gradually.
11.5	Pass around a gate to the paved parking area at Windy Ridge Viewpoint, where you can take in the view and relax before turning around and heading back on the same route.
23.0	Return to Ape Canyon Trailhead.

Norway Pass Trail
Out-and-Back

Location: Blast zone on Mount St. Helens.

Distance: 13.4 miles.

Time: 2 to 3 hours.

Tread: 13.4 miles singletrack.

Season: Summer and fall.

Aerobic level: Moderate to strenuous.

Technical difficulty: 3+.

Hazards: Some loose tread and steep sections.

Highlights: This trail is great for viewing the contrast between the normal forestlands and the blast zone resulting from the May 1980 eruption. Along the way you'll ride some fun singletrack and have good opportunities for wildlife viewing.

Land status: Gifford Pinchot National Forest—Mount St. Helens National Volcanic Monument.

Maps: *Mountain Biking Southwest Washington*—Fat Tire Publications; USGS Spirit Lake East

Access: From Portland take Interstate 5 north 21 miles from the Columbia River Bridge to Washington Highway 503. Head east on WA 503 for 47 miles to Forest Service 25, then take FS 25 north 33 miles to FS 99. Turn west on

•Norway Pass Trail Out-and-Back

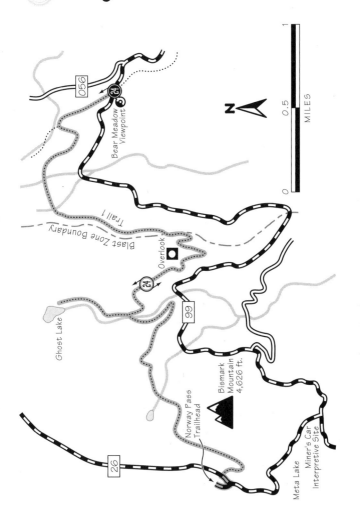

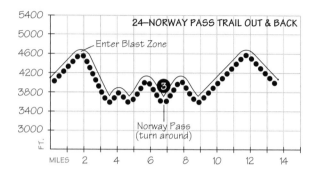

5400
5000
4600
4200
3800
3400
3000

24—NORWAY PASS TRAIL OUT & BACK

Enter Blast Zone

3

Norway Pass
(turn around)

FT.

MILES   2   4   6   8   10   12   14

FS 99 and procede 4.8 miles to Bear Meadow Viewpoint
(2.5 hours from Portland).

The Ride

0.0 From the Bear Meadow Viewpoint cross FS 99 and
pick up Boundary Trail 1 as it begins climbing up a
creek drainage through a thick forest.

0.5 Trail junction, head left on Trail 1 as it continues
climbing and then traverses a steep slope.

1.5 Begin entering the blast zone as the trail angles gently down a ridgeline.

2.4 Negotiate a series of switchbacks as the trail drops
down from the ridge into the Clearwater Creek
drainage.

3.7 Trail junction; head right on a short out-and-back
to view the quiet beauty of Ghost Lake.

4.2 Reach Ghost Lake; turn around at this point and
head back to the last junction.

4.7 Head right at the trail junction and continue on
Trail 1 as it climbs up to a low plateau below
Bismark Mountain.

6.0 Begin traversing down a steep slope as the trail heads toward the Norway Pass Trailhead.

6.7 Norway Pass Trailhead. Take a break here before heading back on the same route (or head back on FS 26 and FS 99 which are narrow, windy, and often busy with traffic).

13.4 Bear Meadow Viewpoint.

Badger Ridge Loop

Location: Dark Divide area east of Mount St. Helens.

Distance: 14.6 miles.

Time: 2.5 to 3.5 hours.

Tread: 5.1 miles singletrack; 4.9 miles doubletrack; 2.8 miles gravel; 1.8 miles pavement.

Season: Summer and fall.

Aerobic level: Strenuous.

Technical difficulty: 4.

Hazards: Some loose tread and steep sections, water ruts on Trail 1, steep hike-a-bike section.

Highlights: A fun but challenging loop. Expect to get the heart rate up as you walk up the steep slope to Badger Ridge. Except for some erosion ruts the trail is fun for biking.

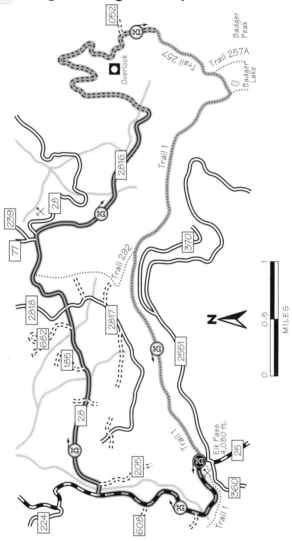

•Badger Ridge Loop

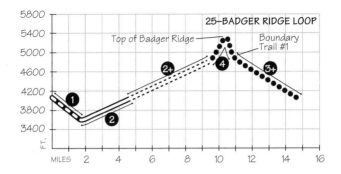

Land status: Gifford Pinchot National Forest—Mount St. Helens National Volcanic Monument.

Maps: *Mountain Biking Southwest Washington*—Fat Tire Publications; USGS French Butte.

Access: From Portland take Interstate 5 north 21 miles from the Columbia River Bridge to Washington Highway 503. Head east on WA 503 for 47 miles to Forest Service 25 then proceed north on FS 25 for 28 miles to Elk Pass (2.5 hours from Portland).

The Ride

0.0 From Elk Pass head north on paved road FS 25 as it drops rapidly.

1.8 Look for gravel road FS 28 on your right; this road meanders easily through an old-growth forest. You will pass several side roads as you continue riding on FS 28.

3.9 Four-way road junction; continue straight on FS 28.

4.6 Five-way road junction; head right on dirt road FS 2816 as it begins climbing easily.

6.4	The road becomes rougher and begins climbing more steeply.
9.1	Junction with FS 052; bear right for a short distance until the road ends.
9.5	Road ends and Trail 257 begins. Start climbing steeply until you can ride no farther, then shoulder your bike for the half-mile hoof to the top of the ridge.
10.1	Reach the top of the ridge and begin descending steeply.
10.2	Look for Trail 257A on the left; this trail climbs steeply to the top of Badger Peak. Continue straight on Trail 257 as it descends toward the Boundary Trail.
10.4	Junction with the Boundary Trail 1; head right as it descends toward Elk Pass.
12.3	Junction with Trail 292; keep left as the trail rises and falls along the ridgeline through a thick forest.
14.6	FS 25 at Elk Pass.

French Butte Loop

Location: Cowlitz River Drainage.

Distance: 17.5 miles.

Time: 2.5 to 3.5 hours.

•French Butte Loop

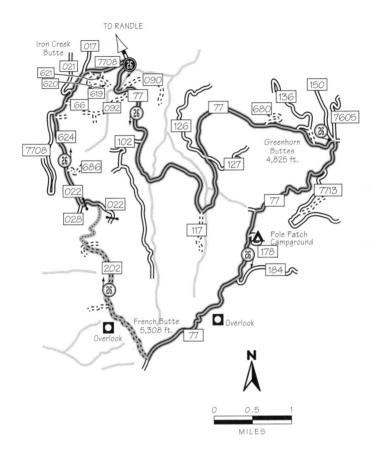

Tread: 1 mile singletrack; 4.8 miles doubletrack; 11.7 miles gravel.

Season: Summer and fall.

Aerobic level: Moderate to strenuous; long gradual climbs.

Technical difficulty: 2+.

Hazards: Watch for vehicles on the road sections; steep but smooth singletrack.

Highlights: A fun and scenic, easy loop. A long climb is rewarded by fast descents on nice riding surfaces.

Land status: Gifford Pinchot National Forest—Mount St. Helens National Volcanic Monument.

Maps: *Mountain Biking Southwest Washington*—Fat Tire Publications; USGS French Butte, Greenhorn Buttes, McCoy Peak, Tower Rock.

Access: From Portland take Interstate 5 north for 68 miles to U.S. Highway 12. Head east on U.S. 12 for 48 miles to Randle, then go south on Forest Service 25 for 1 mile to FS 23 on the left. Follow FS 23 for 8.5 miles to FS 28 on your right and follow FS 28 for 3 miles to FS 76 on your left. Follow FS 76 for 2.8 miles to FS 77 on your left, then follow this 7.8 miles to the junction with FS 7708 where the pavement ends. Begin your ride here (3 hours from Portland).

The Ride

0.0 Begin by riding uphill on gravel road FS 77; be sure your seat height is correct and stamina strong because this is the beginning of a 12-mile climb.

2.1 Pass through the first of several small creek drainages.

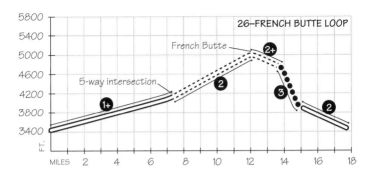

5.8 Begin climbing more steeply.

7.2 Five-way intersection; head right on FS 77 as it turns into a dirt road and continues to climb.

9.5 Notice the access road for Pole Patch Campground on the left; continue straight. The views continue to open up as you climb.

12.0 Junction with doubletrack FS 202 at the top of the climb; head right as this jeep road drops away from French Butte.

13.7 As the road begins to round a bend to the left, look for Trail 254 on the right, which leaves the road as a doubletrack then immediately turns left and becomes a singletrack. The trail, which is wide and well graded, drops rapidly down a steep sidehill slope.

14.7 Junction with gravel road FS 022 across from a fenced tree farm; head left and continue downhill.

15.0 Junction with FS 028 on the left; bear right past several more road junctions.

16.2 Junction with FS 7708; head right back toward your car.

17.5 Return to the junction with FS 77.

27

Krause Ridge Loop

Location: Cispus River Drainage.

Distance: 5.8 miles.

Time: 1 to 2 hours.

Tread: 3.4 miles singletrack; 2.4 miles doubletrack.

Season: Summer and fall.

Aerobic level: Moderate.

Technical difficulty: 2+.

Hazards: Occasional switchbacks and logs along the trail.

Highlights: Great singletrack through a mature lowland forest and nice views of the Cispus River Valley.

Land status: Gifford Pinchot National Forest—Cowlitz Valley Ranger District.

Maps: *Mountain Biking Southwest Washington*—Fat Tire Publications; USGS Greenhorn Buttes.

Access: From Portland, take Interstate 5 north 68 miles to U.S. Highway 12. Head east on U.S. 12 for 48 miles to Randle. From there go south on Forest Service 25 for 6.5 miles to FS 2506 on the left. Follow this road 2.3 miles to its junction with FS 037, park here (2.5 to 3 hours from Portland).

•Krause Ridge Loop

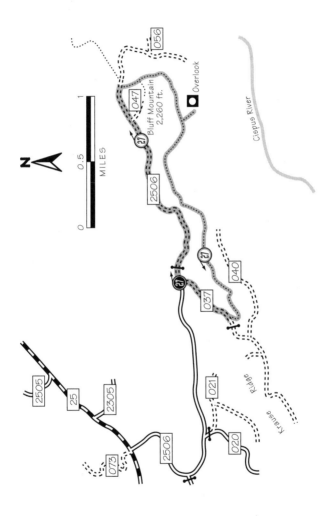

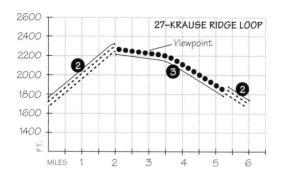

The Ride

0.0 After parking continue up FS 2506 as it climbs steeply up Bluff Mountain.

1.5 As the road begins to level out look for FS 047 on your right; continue straight.

1.9 Look for the Krause Ridge Trail 275 as it crosses the road. Head right on singletrack as the trail climbs gradually on well-maintained trail.

2.2 Stay left at a junction with a faint trail.

3.0 Head left at a three-way trail junction; follow this side trail to its end at a great viewpoint of the Cispus River Valley.

3.1 Viewpoint; turn around and head back to the main trail.

3.2 Back at the three-way intersection, head left as the trail begins a fun descent.

4.7 Begin a series of easily negotiated switchbacks as the trail continues to drop.

5.3 Junction with doubletrack FS 037; head right back down to your car.

5.8 Return to car.

Elochman Loop

Location: Elochman River Valley.

Distance: 7 miles.

Time: 1 to 2 hours.

Tread: 4.1 miles singletrack; 1.9 miles doubletrack; 1 mile gravel.

Season: Spring, summer, and fall.

Aerobic level: Moderate.

Technical difficulty: 3+.

Hazards: Watch for ATVs on the road sections; rooted singletrack; very slick conditions on the doubletrack and singletrack when wet.

Highlights: A fun but demanding short loop. It's best to ride up here when the ground is dry, which severely limits the number of available riding days.

Land status: Washington Department of Natural Resources.

Maps: *Mountain Biking Southwest Washington*—Fat Tire Publications; USGS Nass Point, Skamokawa Pass.

Access: From Portland take Interstate 5 north 36 miles to the Long Beach exit onto U.S. Highway 4. Go through Longview and then go another 30 miles to Elochman Valley Road. Turn right onto Elochman Valley Road and drive 3.8 miles to Beaver Creek Road. Turn right onto Beaver Creek Road and go 4.6 miles to Road 1000. Turn left onto 1000

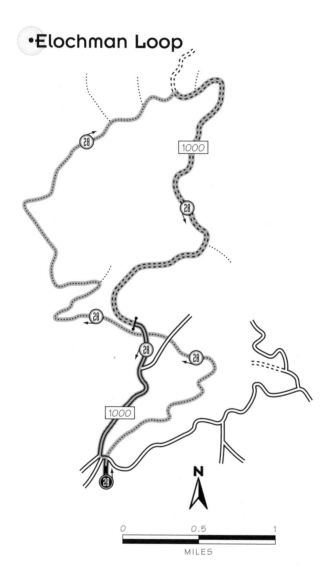

•Elochman Loop

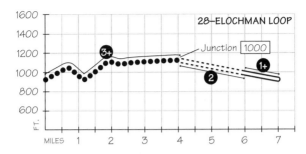

and drive 1.9 miles to the Bradley Biking Trail and Recreation Area parking area on the right.

The Ride

0.0 Leave the parking area and look for the trail, which begins just across the access road; begin the roller-coaster singletrack as it winds through dense forest.

1.1 After a steep descent, cross a gravel road.

1.2 Cross another gravel road near a gate.

1.4 The trail touches the gravel road briefly and then heads back into the forest.

2.0 Look for a faint singletrack on the right; keep left as the trail continues to roll through the forest.

3.7 Bear right at a trail junction.

3.9 Again, keep right at a trail junction.

4.1 Intersect dirt road 1000; head right on this wide ATV route.

6.0 Round a vehicle barrier and continue riding down road 1000 as it turns to gravel.

6.2 Notice a gravel road that junctions in on the left; continue straight.

6.9 Reach a four-way intersection, head left back into the parking area.

7.0 Trailhead.

A Short Index of Rides

Road Rides
(includes jeep tracks and unmaintained routes)
>Leif Erikson Drive Out-and-Back
>Still Creek Out-and-Back
>Barlow Road
>Bennett Pass Road Out-and-Back
>Lone Butte Loop
>French Butte Loop

Sweet Singletrack Rides
(may also include road and doubletrack portions)
>Historic Hiking Trail
>Henry Hagg Lake Trail
>Powell Butte
>Molalla River Corridor Trails
>Old Salmon River Trail
>Gunsight/Gumjuwac Loop
>Umbrella Falls/Sahalie Falls Loop
>Tarbell Trail Loop
>Three Corner Rock
>Siouxan Creek Out-and-Back
>Lewis River Trail Out-and-Back
>Ape Canyon/Plains of Abraham Out-and-Back
>Norway Pass Trail Out-and-Back

Beginner's Luck
>Leif Erikson Drive Out-and-Back
>Still Creek Out-and-Back
>Old Man Pass Loop
>Lone Butte Loop
>Krause Ridge Loop

Technical Tests

Historic Hiking Trail
Molalla River Corridor Trails
Gunsight/Gumjuwac Loop
Umbrella Falls/Sahalie Falls Loop
Larch Mountain Loop
Three Corner Rock
Badger Ridge Loop

Great Climbs—The Yearn to Burn

Long Firelane Loop
The Wildside of Forest Park
Bennett Pass Road Out-and-Back
Larch Mountain Loop
Tarbell Trail Loop
Three Corner Rock
Ape Canyon/Plains of Abraham Out-and-Back
Badger Ridge Loop
French Butte Loop

Great Downhills

The Wildside of Forest Park
Barlow Road
Bennett Pass Road Out-and-Back
Larch Mountain Loop
French Butte Loop

Glossary

ATB: All-terrain bicycle; a.k.a. mountain bike, sprocket rocket, fat tire flyer.

ATV: All-terrain vehicle; in this book ATV refers to motor-bikes and three- and four-wheelers designed for off-road use.

Bail: Getting off the bike, usually in a hurry, whether or not you mean to. Often a last resort.

Bunny hop: Leaping up, while riding, and lifting both wheels off the ground to jump over an obstacle (or for sheer joy).

Clean: To ride without touching a foot (or other body part) to the ground; to ride a tough section successfully.

Clipless: A type of pedal with a binding that accepts a special cleat on the soles of bike shoes. The cleat clicks in for more control and efficient pedaling, and out for safe landings (in theory).

Contour: A line on a topographic map showing a continuous elevation level over uneven ground. Also used as a verb to indicate a fairly easy or moderate grade: "The trail contours around the west flank of the mountain before the final grunt to the top."

Dab: To put a foot or hand down (or hold on to or lean on a tree or other support) while riding. If you have to dab, then you haven't ridden that piece of trail **clean.**

Downfall: Trees that have fallen across the trail.

Doubletrack: A trail, jeep road, ATV route, or other track with two distinct ribbons of **tread,** typically with grass growing in between. No matter which side you choose, the other rut always looks smoother.

Endo: Lifting the rear wheel off the ground and riding (or abruptly not riding) on the front wheel only. Also known, at various degrees of control and finality, as a nose wheelie, "going over the handlebars," and a face plant.

Fall line: The angle and direction of a slope; the **line** you follow when gravity is in control and you aren't.

Graded: When a gravel road is scraped level to smooth out the washboards and potholes, it has been *graded*. In this book, a road is listed as graded only if it is regularly maintained. Not all such roads are graded every year, however.

Granny gear: The innermost and smallest of the three chainrings on the bottom bracket spindle (where the pedals and crank arms attach to the bike's frame). Shift down to your granny gear (and up to the biggest cog on the rear hub) to find your lowest (easiest) gear for climbing.

Hammer: To ride hard; derived from how it feels afterward: "I'm hammered."

Hammerhead: Someone who actually enjoys feeling **hammered.** A Type A personality rider who goes hard and fast all the time.

Kelly hump: An abrupt mound of dirt across the road or trail. These are common on old logging roads and skidder tracks, placed there to block vehicle access. At high speeds, they become launching pads for bikes and inadvertent astronauts.

Line: The route (or trajectory) between or over obstacles or through turns. **Tread** or trail refers to the ground you're riding on; the line is the path you choose within the tread (and exists mostly in the eye of the beholder).

Off-the-seat: Moving your butt behind the bike seat and over the rear tire; used for control on extremely steep descents. This position increases braking power, helps prevent **endos,** and reduces skidding.

Portage: To carry the bike, usually up a steep hill, across unrideable obstacles, or through a stream.

Quads: Thigh muscles (short for quadriceps); or maps in the USGS topographic series (short for quadrangles). Nice quads of either kind can help get you out of trouble in the backcountry.

Ratcheting: Also known as backpedaling; pedaling backward to avoid hitting rocks or other obstacles with the pedals.

Sidehill: Where the trail crosses a slope. If the **tread** is narrow, keep your inside (uphill) pedal up to avoid hitting the ground. If the **tread** tilts downhill, you may have to use some body language to keep the bike plumb or vertical to avoid slipping out.

Singletrack: A trail, game run, or other track with only one ribbon of **tread.** But this is like defining an orgasm as a muscle cramp. Good singletrack is pure fun.

Spur: A side road or trail that splits off from the main route.

Surf: Riding through loose gravel or sand, when the wheels sway from side to side. Also *heavy surf:* frequent and difficult obstacles.

Suspension: A bike with front suspension has a shock-absorbing fork or stem. Rear suspension absorbs shock between the rear wheel and frame. A bike with both is said to be fully suspended.

Switchbacks: When a trail goes up a steep slope, it zigzags or *switchbacks* across the **fall line** to ease the gradient of the climb. Well-designed switchbacks make a turn with at least an 8-foot radius and remain fairly level within the turn itself. These are rare, however, and cyclists often struggle to ride through sharply angled, sloping switchbacks.

Track stand: Balancing on a bike in one place, without rolling forward appreciably. Cock the front wheel to one side and bring that pedal up to the one or two o'clock position. Now control your side-to-side balance by applying pressure on the pedals and brakes and changing the angle of the front wheel, as needed. It takes practice but really comes in handy at stoplights, on switchbacks, and when trying to free a foot before falling.

Tread: The riding surface, particularly regarding **singletrack.**

Water bar: A log, rock, or other barrier placed in the **tread** to divert water off the trail and prevent erosion. Peeled logs can be slippery and cause bad falls, especially when they angle sharply across the trail.

About the Author

Scott Rapp lives in Salem, Oregon, with his wife, Amy, and yellow lab, Henry. He is the owner of Adventure Maps, Inc., a publisher of waterproof mountain biking and cross-country skiing maps for various locations throughout the West. Running this company keeps Scott involved in mountain biking and the trail issues that the sport is facing. Scott also works full-time as an account executive for R/H/A/S Advertising and Public Relations.